Thank you for being a part of

THE PLACEHOLDER !! :)

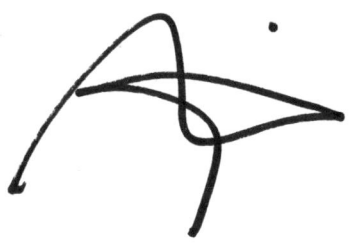

Thank you for
being a part of
it!! :)

THE PLACEHOLDER

THE PLACE TO GO TO CREATE
YOUR NOBLE WORK

MIROO KIM

MANUSCRIPTS
PRESS

COPYRIGHT © 2025 MIROO KIM
All rights reserved.

The manufacturer's authorized representative in the EU for product safety is: Authorised Rep Compliance Ltd, 71 Lower Baggot Street, Dublin D02 P593 Ireland (www.arccompliance.com)

THE PLACEHOLDER
The Place to Go to Create Your Noble Work

ISBN   979-8-88926-433-0   *Paperback*
            979-8-88926-434-7   *Hardcover*
            979-8-88926-432-3   *Ebook*

To Dad, who loved me endlessly from day one of my life.

To Ozz, who expands my love every day.

To Dan, who humbles me infinitely with love.

Table of Contents

INTRODUCTION. THE MOMENT OF TRUTH — 11

PART 1
CHAPTER 1. TWO BIG MISTAKES WE MAKE ABOUT CAREER — 21
CHAPTER 2. WHAT'S AT STAKE FOR US? — 35

PART 2
CHAPTER 3. WELCOME TO THE PLACEHOLDER! — 55
CHAPTER 4. THE FIRST PERSPECTIVE: BE LIKE AN ANTHROPOLOGIST TO LEARN ABOUT YOURSELF — 67
CHAPTER 5. THE SECOND PERSPECTIVE: BE LIKE A DESIGNER TO IDEATE YOURSELF — 79
CHAPTER 6. THE THIRD PERSPECTIVE: BE LIKE A MAD SCIENTIST TO EXPERIMENT WITH IDEAS — 95
CHAPTER 7. THE ILLUSIVE OBSTACLES OF THE PLACEHOLDER — 111

PART 3
CHAPTER 8. FROM THE PLACEHOLDER TO NOBLE WORK — 125
CHAPTER 9. GRADUATING FROM THE PLACEHOLDER — 139

CONCLUSION — 153
ACKNOWLEDGMENTS — 159
NOTES — 163

*In life when one door closes, another door always opens…
but the hallways are a bitch.*

—RONNIE KAYE, *Spinning Straw into Gold*

INTRODUCTION
The Moment of Truth

Have you seen children crying out of control on a bus or train? What about a thirty-seven-year-old woman?

I was that woman. One day in 2016, I wept for the entire sixty-five minutes straight on the shuttle ride from work. The shuttle bus was almost always quiet, full of Meta employees either busy working on their laptops or preoccupied on their phones. Although I did my best to muffle the sound, I must have made everyone around me feel awkward, including the poor engineer next to me. He squinted at me from time to time while coding, but I couldn't have cared less. No, this wasn't how I behaved in public. This had never happened before.

What had caused this? Right before getting on the shuttle, I was in a meeting with a senior executive and his team to talk about the project I led. The executive didn't even look at me while I talked. With his eyes glued to the laptop screen, he kept busy typing away. I tried reading his face, but there was nothing to read. Even before I finished my last sentence, he blurted out, "This is a complete waste of time. I don't think we should do this." Then he left the meeting.

Ouch.

Sure, it hurt, but I used to shrug it off and move on. This kind of work friction was common. What triggered my tears wasn't the VP's bluntness. Deep down, I could feel something else, more than anger or frustration from work. During the entire bus ride from work, I kept thinking, *I cannot do this anymore,* mixed with tears. I'd had enough.

But enough of what? What do I want to stop doing?

As I got off the shuttle and walked back home, it occurred to me that the VP had actually pointed out a truth in a way: I was wasting my life. To him, the project was a waste of time because he couldn't find any value in it. To me, my job was a waste of time because I couldn't find it meaningful anymore.

In fact, this sense of emptiness had been percolating for some years, but I had to admit I kept ignoring it. I couldn't comprehend it because I was living the life I wanted—at least I thought so. I had attended great schools. I had ventured to the US from Korea to work in Silicon Valley. Working at Apple, Microsoft, and Meta, I built an amazing résumé for fifteen years, a career many people strive for. My work brought me all around the world—from Africa to Europe, Asia, and Latin America—with all kinds of exotic experiences and surrounded me with incredibly smart and remarkable people.

I felt as if I had become an ungrateful, spoiled child. *With this ridiculous amount of privilege, I must not feel this way,* I thought. What made this emptiness even more perplexing and exasperating was I had already tried many things to *fix* it.

I had changed jobs or moved to a different company. I took on more responsibilities in leadership, hoping a new challenge would make a difference. I took time off work so I could rest and prevent burnout. I built new habits, such as meditation and running, and learned new skills through many self-development courses. I was in therapy for depression too. However, the emptiness remained. I was dealing with some insatiable longing. But longing for what? I couldn't figure out what I was looking for.

When I got to my apartment, still shaken and confused, one thing was clear. I wanted to stop suffering from this emptiness. Quitting this job and looking for a new one or going on another exotic vacation wouldn't do anymore.

That playbook was old; I desperately needed a completely different playbook this time.

THE PLACEHOLDER: CREATING (NOT FINDING) WHAT YOU ARE LOOKING FOR

After that day of ugly crying on the shuttle, I started testing out random ideas I had never tried before. Because I didn't know what I was looking for, nor where to look for it, in the beginning, it looked pretty much like throwing spaghetti on a wall to see what stuck.

That period of my career was intensely experimental, with many hypotheses, small and big tests, and tons of insights. Like an anthropologist, I discovered and learned a lot about myself and what mattered to me. Like a designer, I constantly came up with new ideas to try. And like a mad scientist, I kept experimenting with those ideas. Some experiments were successful and some were disappointing. Nonetheless, those experiences helped me gather insights for the next new ideas and tests.

Roughly five years into this experimental period I named the "Placeholder," I finally crafted the right "input" for it, the work that became so meaningful to me. For the first time in my life, beyond the sense of fulfillment, there was contentment and joy from work that deeply aligned with my values. No more emptiness.

What is a "placeholder"? You probably have seen it in a digital template of documents like a newsletter. A placeholder is a symbol, word, or piece of text used to temporarily hold the place of an actual item or data in a document, where content is yet to be provided or finalized. Here is one of the common examples of a placeholder, which usually starts with "Lorem ipsum."[1]

Image by Miroo Kim

A placeholder serves various purposes depending on the context. In graphic and web design, placeholders—often grayed boxes or dummy text like "Lorem ipsum" above—show where images, text, or other elements will be placed before the actual content is available. In programming or software development, a placeholder can be a variable, identifier, or parameter that stores a temporary value that will be replaced by the actual data when the program runs.

In mathematical formulas, a placeholder can represent a variable or an unspecified value that will be defined later.

As you can tell from the general use of placeholders, the "Placeholder" in the context of our work serves the same purposes. The Placeholder is an in-between period we enter to create a new *input* for our career with novel ideas and experiments because whatever we've been doing no longer serves us.

In most challenges with our career, we think we know where we want to be. We set the destination first, such as how to get a job at company A, how to become a marketer or whether to become a lawyer or a dancer. And all we need to do is figure out the route—how to get there. But in the Placeholder, the destination or end point is unknown. We don't know where we want to be, and we only get to know it as we go; it's a wicked problem. The only way to solve this is to be open to as many new ideas as possible, test them in a quick and dirty way, and constantly reiterate. This mindset is essential in the Placeholder.

More than the meaningful work I created as a result of the Placeholder, what fascinated me most was the experience itself. The experience was absolutely different from what I used to do in the past—simply searching for a job or changing to a different career that already existed. Curious to learn if there were other people who had similar experiences as mine, I collected hidden Placeholder stories of some of the most successful people in history. By interviewing various people who had gone through or were going through the Placeholders, I recognized some common elements in their experiences. Delving into literature and research of psychology, neuroscience, philosophy, economics, and history, I could put together the three most important perspectives to consider in the Placeholder.

Many situations and reasons might prompt you to enter the Placeholder. You might be bored to death with your current work, or you have lost interest or meaning in your lifelong career, like I did. Maybe you are forced to leave your job because of layoffs. Whatever the reasons are, it's easy to get anxious and worried because it seems as if you are deviating. This sense of getting sidetracked can make you fall back to the old pattern out of fear, making you look for a similar job again or move to a different company for more or less the same work. Often, you intentionally ignore that urge to do something fundamentally different about the situation, hoping everything will be fine.

But it's not fine. I know it because I tried all of those, and none of them helped but put me back to where I was—emptiness. Even worse, it activated an internal saboteur, and I criticized myself for not knowing how to figure it out. All my life, the question I asked myself was "What do I want to do?" But I was facing a new question I never asked myself: "What matters to me?" This question urged me to create my own path rather than following what was already available. This problem was a brand-new one I never learned how to solve at business school or in any career coaching.

We are so well trained to search for a job or aim our career in a slightly different direction. Thousands of books and YouTube channels exist about it. But what if none of them really work for us? What if what we find meaningful is something new that doesn't exist yet? How do we break the mold and create our own career based on what truly matters to us? What is at stake with it? What does it take to do it? These questions compelled me to write this book.

IT'S AN OPPORTUNITY, NOT A CRISIS

What am I doing here? Am I living the life I want? What do I even want? Encountering these questions after building a great career you thought you wanted could be completely debilitating and perplexing. You may think you cannot afford to act like this, you are too old to have these questions now, or you are too young to have a so-called midlife crisis.

Such reactions are legitimate and understandable. However, you are neither too old to ask these questions nor having a midlife crisis. You are allowed to question what you have been doing. Doing so is not a crisis but a great opportunity for you to look into your new "why" for work so you can live a life truly meaningful to you.

It takes great effort and courage to enter the Placeholder of self-discovery, radical ideas, and nonstop experiments. Feeling uncertain and anxious about it? Nervously excited? Super curious and hopeful? All of those belong in the Placeholder. Don't worry. You will be in good company with me and many others who have been or are currently walking in the Placeholder. We'll walk together.

Let's step into it.

PART 1

CHAPTER 1

Two Big Mistakes We Make about Career

WHAT DO YOU WANT TO BE WHEN YOU GROW UP?
A couple of years ago, my stepdaughter reached the first big milestone of her life: kindergarten graduation. At the graduation ceremony, all the kids were asked to talk about what they wanted to be when they grew up. My wide-eyed stepdaughter waited for her turn, listening carefully to what her classmates presented. When the teacher finally passed the microphone to her, she stood up and spoke in a clear and loud voice. "When I grow up, I want to be a ballerina in the morning and the evening, a gymnast in the afternoon, and a paleontologist, ice skater, and many other things too."

Image by Miroo Kim

With a big smile on her face, she strode back to her seat to a round of applause. As a parent, it was such a memorable moment of pride, joy, and love for her. What fascinated me most was her idea about work. She wanted to try out and do so many things; why not say them all?

Think about it. All of us were like that when we were little. To the classic question by grown-ups—"What do you want to be when you grow up?"—my answer as a kid changed multiple times from being Madonna—I wanted to literally be her—to an Olympic swimmer, a diplomat, and ten other things. I wasn't tied to a single career track, nor did I identify myself with a single job, until I got older and went to college.

I don't deny that it takes a lot of time and effort to build each career, and working in multiple careers at the same time is challenging, of course. But why do we assume we should work in only one career from the moment of graduating college until we retire? What has this single-career perspective done to us?

Nothing is wrong with focusing on building one career. Working in marketing at Apple, I saw the joy on the faces of people as they played with iPods or iMacs for the first time. Every time was priceless. What about those times when I was analyzing and forecasting the demands of the new iPhones that no one knew about yet?

I had countless moments when I got to see the power of technology too. On one research trip, I got to meet a woman living in the rural area of Brazil with poor cellular connection. She was so thankful for WhatsApp's voice message because using it was the only way to stay in touch with her son working in Sao Paulo. She was illiterate, and she couldn't depend on phone calls due to the poor cell service in the area. Technology was a lifesaver for her to stay connected with her loved ones.

Working at the forefront of the latest technologies and seeing how they changed the lives of people was exhilarating and meaningful, but that sense of meaning with my tech career didn't last. Yet, I kept going on with my career track for two reasons. First, I had already invested so much time and effort into it, so it seemed irrational to start over. Second, I had no idea where to start and what to do to change to a different career. It seemed like an insurmountable task, so I kept pretending my career was still meaningful to me and everything was fine, although in reality, I had to drag myself to work every day.

MISTAKE ONE: ONE CAREER FOR ONE LIFE?

Image by Miroo Kim

Culturally and socially in the US, we are not well prepared to pursue different career tracks throughout life. In college, we choose one or maybe double majors based on the assumption that it'll determine our career for life. This expectation poses a threat to many liberal arts majors, as we assume there is less definitive connection to future careers.

Afraid this uncertainty might obscure the future for their children, parents recommend they go into practical majors such as business, economics, premed, or STEM (science, technology, engineering, and mathematics). Interestingly, this contributed to the explosion of double majors in elite universities, according to some research. As high as 40 percent of students said they chose one major to satisfy their parents and another for their own interests of learning.[1]

The problem is not the number of majors or choosing a certain career track at any point. We always have to choose something at some point, but the issue is the obsession with a single career throughout our life. This can present two problems: One, it makes us over-identify ourselves with our careers, and two, it makes us inflexible when what matters to us changes.

Five years after starting my career at Apple, I decided to pursue an MBA degree. I wanted to complement my undergraduate liberal arts degree with business and have some time to explore other options I didn't know yet. However, pretty much from day one at business school, my classmates and I had to narrow down the career track we wanted to focus on—consulting, finance, tech, marketing, etc.—for two years, like we had to do in college.

At the end of the first year, once we got internships in the field we chose, we mostly stayed on the same path in the second year. As we secured the full-time offers in the career track we chose in the beginning of the school, we assumed it would be the only career we had post-MBA and zeroed in on striving for it only. We had no class or discussion about what to do in case we wanted to alter our careers after business school or how to navigate through potential changes in what we valued in the long term. Thinking about various other paths we could take meant indecisiveness, which wasn't a virtue in business school. "Keep your eyes on the target" was the mantra.

Just like that, we became a career. And because of that, we also made ourselves vulnerable to whatever happened to our jobs. We were constantly anxious about how we were doing. That was the problem with self-identification. One of my business school friends used to say, "My work defines me," and my friends and I used to nod in agreement. We subconsciously accepted being laser-focused on a single career as a ticket to success and, therefore, a happy life. This assumption made us live in constant anxiety and worry over our *one and only* career, no matter how successful we became.

Ultimately, this obsessive focus on a single career made us inflexible with changes when our *one and only* careers stopped serving us. The tech career I built with intense focus and investment was not meaningful anymore after about ten years. After taking all the actions I could think of, such as changing roles, teams, and even companies, I had the same flatness.

Although I couldn't put my finger on it exactly, I knew something deep inside me changed. I didn't know whether it was my strengths, weaknesses, aspirations, goals, values, or something else. It felt like a part of me I never paid attention to was trying really hard to speak up; however, I couldn't hear it. That part of me was silenced by the dogma of "one career for one life" that I was so deeply conditioned by.

It turned out I wasn't the only one who suffered from this. I started confessing to my close friends how stifling it was to keep going with my career as it was. To my surprise, many of my friends, who looked all very successful on the outside, shared similar frustrations secretly, one by one. We were so damn well trained at pursuing a single career, dedicating ten, fifteen or sometimes twenty years, but were never prepared for what to do when it stopped serving us.

This created so much tension and conflict in our work life. We were less engaged at work and constantly unsatisfied. People around us noticed that too. We complained more, but we were guilty at the same time exactly for that because everything looked *perfect* on the surface. It was a predicament. Most of all, we were so confused and unsettled. As faithful students to the dogma of the obsessive focus on a single career, we never assumed we might someday want to change. The result of this inflexibility was eating us from the inside.

The peculiar point in the way we reason our career is that it's all deductive. Rather than discovering and creating through many empirical examples, we start with a conclusion. The classic question "What do you want to be when you grow up?" is a great example. By declaring what we want to be first, we naturally conclude our future in a singular way. The underlying assumptions that our college major would determine our career, and we would never want to change from it, pressure us to hold on to that conclusion. Then another adage, "follow your passion," only reinforces this overly deductive way of thinking about career—and makes it even more limiting.

FOLLOW YOUR PASSION AND GET STUCK WITH IT

Find a job that you enjoy doing, and you will never have to work a day in your life.

—ANONYMOUS

You have probably read or heard this phrase in many self-help books, on Instagram posts, or in graduation commencement speeches. Another popular version of this career advice is to *follow your passion*. It sounds like great advice, but Carol S. Dweck and her colleagues at Stanford University have discovered in their research that it can hold back your life satisfaction due to its narrow-mindedness and dedication to a single passion.[2] This seemingly helpful advice is actually loaded with so many unhelpful assumptions.

Image by Miroo Kim

One, it presumes you already know what your passion is. Your passions and interests are preformed, so you simply need to discover them. However, most people need to learn and expose themselves to different jobs and companies over time in order to develop their interests and passions. In other words, your passions are what you get to learn about only after you go through different experiences. It can be a source of tremendous stress and anxiety in case you believe you need to define your passion first.

Two, it assumes you will have only one passion in life. You are multidimensional and evolving as you go through different experiences in many life stages. You will have more than one interest and passion in life. Also, your passion might change too. Therefore, if you focus on a single career based on one passion or interest, you will leave no room for other passions and interests to be discovered and developed.

And three, it makes you less resilient at work. "Follow your passion" creates the illusion that a "dream job" is waiting for you somewhere, and once you find it, everything will be easy. In their research, Dweck and her colleagues discovered that the level of engagement at work tanked significantly more for those who strongly believed in "follow your passion" when they encountered issues at work. They concluded that "Urging people to find their passion may lead them to put all their eggs in one basket but then to drop that basket when it becomes difficult to carry."³

In one way, the "follow your passion" mantra makes sense on the surface. It restates the main purpose of work as to satisfy individuals, not to treat them like a cog in a wheel to maximize profits, as it was for factory workers in the nineteenth century. But can you say things got better if you continue to feel stuck with your career under the name of "the passion?" Before we further contemplate this, it's worth tracing back how the obsessive focus on a single career originated in the history of work.

THE HISTORY OF SPECIALIZATION

In his magnum opus in 1776, *An Inquiry into the Nature and Causes of the Wealth of Nations*, Adam Smith introduces the concept of division of labor, which became a critical foundation for the manufacturing business during the Industrial Revolution.⁴ Factories needed better efficiency with workers. To produce more, the owners of factories couldn't run it like an artisan shop from the medieval times. Smith took a pin factory as an example; a factory could produce forty-eight thousand pins a day with only ten workers when each of them focused on a single task. This practice was such a contrast to the twenty pins the same number of workers of an artisan shop could make in a day.⁵

By dividing labor into different parts and giving one part to each worker, factories could maximize productivity. But why would anyone want to work in that pin factory, doing the same job, such as cutting the wire or putting heads on pins every minute, hour, and day, repeatedly? It sounds awfully boring.

Adam Smith agreed; of course, people wouldn't enjoy working in that pin factory. In fact, he assumed people wouldn't enjoy working anywhere, anyway, because people were *lazy* by nature. The only reason people would do any kind of work was for what they would get paid in return. Smith argued it didn't matter which work they did, as long as they got adequate reward.[6]

In the early twentieth century, Henry Ford further amplified this doctrine with his innovation in the manufacturing model. He implemented the assembly line for the first time in the Ford factory for the mass production of automobiles. What made this assembly line unique was that it was *moving*. The moving assembly line was much more efficient because it took the job to workers who specialized in a single, repetitive task rather than the worker moving to and around the vehicle.[7] This method dramatically increased the speed and efficiency of production, embodying the principles of the division of labor Adam Smith had identified more than a century earlier.

So, we continued to adopt this doctrine of specialization for the maximum efficiency in everything we did. It is applied at the societal level; when everyone performs their role well in their place, society runs like a well-oiled machine. This is also applied to higher education and career; get a job for the degree you earned and focus on building your career with it.

The question we ought to ask is if this still holds true in the twenty-first-century knowledge industry. Does it serve us in a world where new technologies like artificial intelligence and advanced machinery automation are used for maximum efficiency? Should we continue to apply the same principle of efficiency to humans? Shouldn't we reassess the old assumptions that we need to specialize in one career? What if what we need now more than ever is the ultimate flexibility to change and create the work unique to each of us as we are evolving?

MISTAKE TWO: THE QUESTION WE FORGOT TO ASK OURSELVES

How many hours do you think we work in our lifetime? According to Gallup, the workplace consulting and global research company, we work 81,396 hours on average in our life.[8] The only thing we spend more time doing other than working is sleeping. Since we spend so much time at work, we hope to feel satisfied and engaged in our work life. However, Gallup's data shows it isn't going that way. In their most recent annual *State of the Global Workplace* report (2024), 77 percent of people are disengaged and unsatisfied at work.[9]

This isn't a surprise to us. The idea that "work sucks" is everywhere. Comedian Drew Carey used to invite people to join his "I hate my job" club. *Everybody is invited, and we meet at the bar after work every day.*[10]

Whether it's Gallup's research or the widespread notion in popular culture, the sense of feeling disengaged and "stuck" in our work is universal. Whatever causes this disengagement, we mostly try to fix this problem by focusing on *what* we work on or *how* we work. But what if what we need to think about is to look into *why* we work in the first place?

When I started experiencing disengagement in my day-to-day work, I also zeroed in on *what* and *how* I was working by changing to a different job, department, or company. What I didn't consider was that *why* I worked could have changed. In the beginning of my tech career, contributing to changing people's lives with technology was thrilling. That became *why* I continued to pursue that career even after business school.

When I finally had to accept that specific reason was not meaningful to me anymore, I still resisted the need to reappraise my motivation as much as possible. Then came the day of ugly crying on the shuttle bus, bringing up the very question I needed to confront after all: *Why am I working?*

Why do you work?

Why do you drag yourself out of your comfortable bed every morning instead of staying in bed? You might say, "Isn't it obvious? I can't just spend the day doing whatever I'd like to do! I have to make a living, pay rent and bills, and support my family!"

Of course. That's what Adam Smith suggested about why humans worked—only for the compensation.[11] But is that it? As long as you get the right reward for your labor and time, are you satisfied?

American social psychologist Barry Schwartz studied why people worked for decades and what motivated them. When you ask people who feel fulfilled by their work, they have a list of long and compelling nonmonetary reasons why they do the work they do, according to him. Money is a necessity, but it's not sufficient for why they work. For example, they work for social interactions. Even when they work alone, they have plenty of opportunities to connect with other people through their work. Most of all, Schwartz says, they work because working is *meaningful*.[12]

In the documentary *Working: What We Do All Day*, a home care worker in Mississippi chose a job to take care of senior citizens, even though she was paid $9 per hour, compared to the other job she could have had at a meat processing factory for $15. Why? "Because I find this work more meaningful than processing chickens," she said. She had worked many other jobs to pay the bills for her family, which was why she worked, but she didn't find it fulfilling. She switched to elder care work because she wanted to learn and grow to run a nursing home for her sick and old relatives in the future.[13] This work was meaningful to her.

The same applies to you. When you realize your intense focus on your current career doesn't serve you anymore, it means your reason for "why you work" has changed too. Why are you where you are now in your career? Sure, it was *your* decision to be where you are now. You were passionate about growing your career in the current field of marketing, accounting, teaching, medicine, etc. The work was meaningful to you then, and you worked hard for it to become what it is today.

At the same time, as you look back on your career, you might realize external factors such as the expectations of your parents and the perception of success defined by society might have heavily influenced your career decisions too. Being conditioned by those factors as you decided your major in college, job applications, and companies or roles you worked is natural. Because it paid well and offered a decent social status so far, you were satisfied with it too, but its meaning might have changed now.

This is the point of entry to the Placeholder. I am not suggesting you should leave your job just because you don't feel engaged right now. We'll explore that together in the chapters in Part 2, so hold that thought. But if you display some of these symptoms at work—being less engaged, feeling less satisfied, being constantly distracted, and grouching more than ever as a result—you need to think about the underlying problem. The issue might not be about what you do; hence, changing your role or moving to a different company will probably not make those symptoms disappear. Rather, the meaning—why you work—has changed, which is normal because we change all the time.

Don't confuse this with a question about *what* you are passionate about or *what* you want to do because those questions can trick you and let you identify a definitive career in haste. This question is about *why*. This inquiry asks us to inspect what we truly find meaningful, different from the past, with fresh eyes. Only thinking about it won't lead you to the answer either. In a way, we don't know what we are looking for; therefore, we need to come up with various hypotheses and test as many ideas and experiments as possible with an open and flexible mind.

*****

Just because you chose to work in one career after college or business school doesn't mean you have to assume it's your career for life. Just because you spent ten, fifteen, or twenty years of your life working in one career doesn't mean you have to force yourself to keep doing it. In this book, I would like you to challenge that obsessive demand to dedicate your life to a single career, especially if it doesn't serve you anymore. That's the first problem I want all of us to be aware of.

Equally, the second problem to be aware of is the possibility of change with why we work. Because of the obsessive focus on a single career and implicit external expectations around you, you probably didn't have to think hard about why you worked or what you found meaningful to you specifically. However, what this moment calls for is you to discover your own answer to the question "Why do I want to work?" with radical honesty and genuine curiosity.

The direct consequence of these two mistakes is we become seriously inflexible in our relationship with our careers, and we end up feeling "stuck." Our relationship with our career is not a static status. It constantly evolves as we and society change too. No single career exists that we are "called" to do or is given to us. It needs to be constantly inspected and recreated, and doing so is critical because so much is at stake for us individually and societally as we face the rapid and unexpected changes in the future of work.

CHAPTER 2

What's at Stake for Us?

It might not look so detrimental to have such an obsessive focus on a single career or to work without clearly knowing why you work. But what if this is a $8.9 trillion problem? What if it obstructs the fundamental well-being at work? The stakes are high not only for individuals but for workplaces and societies if we do not change.

Let's explore what's at stake through some stories, starting with mine.

The lousiest year in my career was 2016. "Lousy" because I was not at all engaged with my work. I looked busy at work, and my performance was okay. But in reality, I was slacking off, doing the bare minimum with detachment. Most of the days at work, I was either daydreaming in endless meetings, aimlessly browsing for other potential jobs, or scrolling through Instagram. Subconsciously, the notion I didn't find my career meaningful sneaked up on me, but I pretended I didn't see it and kept going as was. My career had gone stale, but I feigned it until that day of the tantrum on the shuttle.

Here's a story from my friend Sam. One day over a drink, he told me, "Have you ever heard the phrase 'What got you here won't get you there'? Now I totally get what that means." He worked in the ad sales of big tech firms for his entire career. "Since I was young, people told me I had great people skills and I was such a persuasive communicator." These qualities benefited him greatly, landing him a job in ad sales at Google right after college, and he was successful in the field for almost two decades.

"Recently, I was let go because of AI (artificial intelligence.) My company doesn't need us humans to sell ads and manage clients anymore; AI can do it better and more efficiently," he said. He could perhaps get a similar job somewhere else, but it didn't seem right to him. "It will be a mistake to stick around with what I was doing because I'd probably get laid off again." Moreover, he didn't find his old job interesting or meaningful anymore. He wanted to do something else. "But I don't know where to start or how to change my career at this point to a completely different direction. It seems almost impossible," confessed Sam with a big sigh.

"My new hire is amazing; he's so savvy with all the technology and full of new ideas," my client, a founder of a startup, told me. She wanted to help this new employee maximize his potential at work, but doing so was not easy. "He always asks me to clarify why his project is worth doing. I appreciate his purpose-driven attitude, and I know that matters to Gen Z. But at the end of the day, what matters to me is whether he gets the job done as expected," she said.

She was skeptical if it was *really* necessary to impose meaning on everything. She wanted to work well with her team, mostly composed of Gen Z, helping them thrive in their career. For her startup to succeed, she desperately needed full commitment from everyone. "It's getting harder to keep my employees deeply engaged at work. I struggle with how to motivate them," she confided.

Do any of these anecdotes sound familiar? If these don't describe your experience, you might have heard or read something similar from people around you or in the media. These stories encapsulate what's at stake for us individually and collectively if we don't address the two big mistakes we talked about in the previous chapter.

COUNTERING DISENGAGEMENT FROM QUIET QUITTING TO GREAT RESIGNATION

My disengagement at work in 2016 would be a perfect example of "quiet quitting." What is quiet quitting? It's a term that first appeared in 2022. Gallup defines it as follows:[1]

> **Quiet quitting:** Employees are filling a seat and watching the clock. They put in the minimum effort required, and they are psychologically disconnected from their employer. Although they are minimally productive, they are more likely to be stressed and burned out than engaged workers because they feel lost and disconnected from their workplace.[2]

Guess how many people are quiet quitting? Tracking how engaged employees are is one way to measure this. Gallup has been tracking employee engagement at workplaces globally since 2009.[3] Employee engagement is considered a leading indicator for company performance, productivity, customer engagement, job satisfaction, and employee retention, etc. So many companies try to improve this metric for this reason. However, it's not been going so well.

In 2009, only 12 percent of the global workforce was feeling engaged at work. It increased slightly every year until 2019, when it rose to 22 percent, but it tanked to 20 percent during the pandemic and has been hovering around 22 to 23 percent since then.[4] To put this into perspective, if one hundred people are working in your company, less than a quarter of people are engaged at work, and the rest are either doing the bare minimum of work or completely checked out. That's a serious problem.

Gallup's research shows that the majority of disengaged employees are quiet quitters. While quiet quitters aren't necessarily as damaging as the *loud* quitters for organizational culture and productivity, quiet quitting is the quintessential disengagement that all organizations need to be concerned about because of its pricey consequences.

What's the societal and economic impact of this low engagement? Gallup estimates that low employee engagement costs the global economy $8.9 trillion or 9 percent of global GDP.[5] This sum is as big as the combined GDPs of China, France, and Germany in 2022.[6] In other words, the cost of low employee engagement globally is equivalent to wiping out the wealth that China, France, and Germany produced in 2022. This loss is the cost of quiet quitting at the societal level.

Individually, quiet quitters are languishing. An organizational psychologist, Adam Grant, defined languishing as a sense of stagnation and emptiness.[7] It feels as if you are muddling through your days and looking at your life through a foggy windshield. Originally, languishing was a term developed by a sociologist, Corey L. M. Keyes, who found that languishing people weren't depressed but weren't thriving either. His research indicated that the people who are languishing right now are most likely to experience major depression and anxiety disorders in the future.[8]

Even worse, in the same Gallup research above, they found out that having a job you hate is worse than being unemployed. Being unsatisfied with your job creates a range of negative emotions, which undermines the overall well-being of life. In short, if you're not engaged at work, you're unlikely to be thriving in life.[9]

Dennis Nørmark and Anders Fogh Jensen confirm a similar impact of disengagement at work in their book *Pseudowork: How We Ended Up Being Busy Doing Nothing*. The authors discovered the disengagement from the lack of meaning at work was a widespread cause of serious health issues. "In Sweden, the number of people suffering stress has exploded, just as it has in Denmark and the rest of Europe; almost

10 percent of the population are on some kind of antidepressant."[10] Roland Paulsen, the sociologist well known for his research on empty work, corroborates this. "Work that is so relentlessly meaningless definitely contributes to a lack of mental well-being. People ask themselves: Is this really how I want to spend my time?"[11]

People were not only quiet quitting but actually left work too, as described in another term, "Great Resignation." The term was coined in May 2021 by Anthony Klots, an associate professor at Texas A&M Mays Business School at the time, to explain the mass exodus of people from work during the pandemic.[12] According to the US Bureau of Labor Statistics, in 2021, over 47 million Americans voluntarily quit their jobs, and in 2022, it rose to 51 million.[13]

At the time, most scholars attributed this mass exit of the workforce mostly to COVID-19 and its direct impact on people, such as health concerns and desire for more flexibility in work conditions. Over the last four years, further research studies by the US Bureau of Labor Statistics, universities, and consulting firms revealed that there were more nuanced underlying reasons for individuals to participate in the Great Resignation.

Harvard researchers found out more people quit their jobs these days mainly because they aren't making the progress they seek in their careers and lives. The *progress* here doesn't mean a steady, linear climb up the corporate ladder, as we used to define it in the past. It's not the job title or how much money you make. Even though you might be promoted at work, if it doesn't mean anything for your personal development, you don't progress.

The progression that matters now is at the intersection of what each individual seeks in professional and personal life.[14] This means the progress is unique to each individual. If the traditional progression meant quantity and security, people today are looking for quality and autonomy, which is more personal.

While the quit rate has tapered a bit to be in line with pre-pandemic level now, these research findings caution in unison that we need to pay attention to these reasons more carefully.[15] Otherwise, more employees will disengage and feign endeavor just to make the day at work more palatable in the short term. They will show up, say all the right things, and pretend to play along; in the meantime, they feel miserable inside, and this will affect their mental well-being, as I experienced.

Imagine seven out of ten people in your team are working in this state, as reported by Gallup. Its collective impact on the culture and productivity of your team and company is colossal.

CAREER-ELASTICITY, THE ULTIMATE SECURITY FROM JOB ANXIETY

Between November 2022 and March 2024, I ran the virtual "Layoff Grief Party." During this time, many small and big tech firms laid off employees on an unprecedented scale, as a cost-cutting effort. About 2,801 companies laid off 581,000 employees globally from 2022 to 2024.[16] This layoff statistic is equivalent to roughly 90 percent of the entire population of Boston, Massachusetts, losing their jobs over two years.[17]

Most of them were internet and software companies including Google, Meta, Amazon, and Microsoft, which over-hired during the pandemic based on the rapid growth expectations.[18] Unfortunately, the expectation didn't hold, and the consumer demand drastically cooled down after the pandemic, so they had to let go of people to survive. The shock waves sent by these inevitable business decisions reverberated through the tech communities.

Abruptly cut off from their jobs, income, and coworkers, the grief people felt was beyond imagination. I wanted to create a space for them to gather and share how they were feeling, no matter which side they were on. Whether they were laid off or saw their teammates let go suddenly, layoff meant loss to everyone. The situation was a collapse of work communities. At this gathering, we welcomed every emotion—from depression, to shock, sadness, cynicism, anger—and grieved together by sharing our experiences.

Although many people who participated in these parties immediately started looking for similar jobs in the same field, a significant number of people strongly wanted to rethink their careers. On average, they had worked in the same career for ten to fifteen years and started losing interest in it anyway. Also, many of them were wary of the impact of rapid technological changes, i.e., artificial intelligence on their careers, like my friend Sam.

This concern is not ungrounded. Adecco Group and Oxford Economics conducted a wide-ranging survey with two thousand executives and thirty-five thousand workers across twenty-seven countries in 2024 about the global workforce of the future. About 41 percent of executives expected to employ fewer people because of technology such as artificial intelligence. About 13 percent of workers said they have lost their jobs because of AI; in 2023, it was only 8 percent. The share of workers who responded that AI has forced them to consider a change of profession increased from 11 percent in 2023 to 21 percent in 2024 as well.[19]

The point is not that we all have to learn how to use artificial intelligence to be prepared for the new career; nor should we be threatened by it. Everything in us and around us is impermanent. It's artificial intelligence now, but there will be something else in the future. What's at stake is our capacity to transform based on what matters to us, not by what happens to us. When we are ready to change based on what matters to us, we have the ultimate shield for our careers from any confusions and worries derived from the macroeconomy or industry in flux.

ORGANIZATIONS CHAINED TO CARROTS AND STICKS

Some people view quiet quitting or the Great Resignation simply as a personal, individual choice, especially the Gen Z workers. Attributing it to a generational difference conveniently makes it an isolated problem for a certain population only, but such a perspective is not helpful for leaders and organizations as a whole.

Fundamentally, quiet quitters want to be engaged with their work and career too. Thinking they are not interested in building a meaningful career simply because they seem to be "coasting" at work at the moment is a huge mistake. They want to be inspired and motivated, but the old version of motivation built in our workplace systems doesn't work for them anymore in this twenty-first century. What's at stake is to understand the new version of motivation rather than trying to maneuver the levers of the old version to get more workers engaged.

In the beginning of human history, our operating model for motivation was survival. We did everything to survive the predators, natural disasters, or anything that would threaten the life of ourselves and species. Daniel Pink, the author of *Drive*, calls this motivation 1.0.[20] As human society developed, our operating model for motivation changed to "reward and punishment." With the Industrial Revolution in the nineteenth century, so many moving parts existed to manage in the industry and society. This led to the invention of the management methods for industrial efficiency, by Frederick Winslow Taylor, also known as the first management consultant.

Taylor proposed that workers were like parts in a complicated machine. If they did their job properly in a timely manner, the machine—factory or company—would operate well. To make sure this happens, you should reward the right behavior and punish the wrong behavior. Daniel Pink calls these extrinsic motivators or "motivation 2.0."[21]

This worked extremely well in the twentieth century. Henry Ford elevated this operating model through the Ford assembly line. Modern organizations, such as order-fulfillment centers and state-of-the-art tech companies, perpetuated this manic emphasis on efficiency. But economies grew far more complex, the nature of work tasks has changed, and we changed too. Now we need a new operating model for motivation, because people inside those institutions aren't engaged much by reward and punishment, as Gallup research showed previously.

Then what does motivation 3.0 entail for the twenty-first century and beyond?

BEYOND CARROTS AND STICKS: UNLOCKING A NEW MOTIVATION MODEL AT WORK IN THE TWENTY-FIRST CENTURY AND BEYOND

Up until I entered the Placeholder, I optimized myself to check all the *boxes* according to the external metrics, such as:

- ☑ Doing well at school with great grades
- ☑ Going to prestigious schools
- ☑ Getting good jobs at respected companies
- ☑ Performing well in my role at work
- ☑ Advancing my career via promotion and more responsibilities

But the Placeholder asked me to pay more attention to my internal metrics, such as what the work meant to me and why it mattered, for the first time in my career. I was aware of the importance of these internal metrics in theory, but I didn't know how to apply them in most career decisions I made in reality.

That changed in the Placeholder. Based on what mattered to me, I ideated and tested those ideas. I had no one else to please but me. This intrinsic motivation became the biggest asset, as I got to develop an internal compass to navigate the nebulous journey of any potential changes in career.

Anyone who enters the Placeholder has an inkling toward this intrinsic motivation. You come to be concerned less with the external rewards and more curious about the inherent satisfaction of the activity itself. The essence of Daniel Pink's motivation 3.0 operating system revolves around the autotelic experiences based on intrinsic motivation. "Autotelic" is from Greek, where "auto" means self and "telos" means goal.[22] Thus, an autotelic activity is done for its own sake, where the process is its own reward. Doing it itself is the goal.

Three elements make a work experience autotelic with motivation 3.0, according to Pink: mastery, autonomy, and purpose.[23]

1. MASTERY

When I signed myself up for two teacher training certification programs simultaneously, doing both while working a demanding full-time job was physically exhausting. Whenever I shared what I was doing with anyone at the time, people gasped in horror and asked how I was managing them all. Some worried I must be burned out.

On the contrary, I rarely felt burned out during that time. Juggling so many things at the same time was indeed challenging, but life was abundant and energizing for me. I was deeply immersed in my experiments and learning more about what I could do to alleviate my own suffering at work. Thinking of some possibilities I could help others in the future with those courses was equally exciting. Of course, it didn't mean everything was perfect. My full-time job was still unsatisfying, but I was growing in the direction that mattered to me. In a way, the dissatisfaction with my career was offset by the sense of growth in the Placeholder.

What I experienced was a sense of mastery. Daniel Pink defines mastery as "the desire to get better and better at something that matters." He writes, "Solving complex problems requires an inquiring mind and the willingness to experiment one's way to a fresh solution. Where motivation 2.0 sought compliance, motivation 3.0 seeks engagement. Only engagement can produce mastery."[24]

I enjoyed getting better with my Placeholder experiment—creating and facilitating team off-sites, workshops, and training leaders to develop emotional intelligence at work. Although that had nothing to do with my full-time job as a business development manager, I did it gladly for various teams and individuals at work in my spare time. In turn, this created a deep sense of engagement at work in general, and I didn't suffer from lack of motivation or languishing anymore even for my full-time job. This gift was quite unexpected.

2. AUTONOMY

Another counterintuitive outcome from the Placeholder was that I performed better in my full-time job even though I didn't enjoy it anymore. Generally, if you aren't satisfied with your job, you disengage and care less. How come I performed better then?

First, the experiments I was running on the side gave me a huge sense of control. I could change little in my work at that time—company, conditions, the job itself, the people I worked with, etc. But for the classes and programs I was offering to various teams and individuals, I was in control.

Secondly, I had to work more effectively to do both my full-time job and the Placeholder experiments; therefore, I prioritized better, laser-focused on what really mattered. Doing both at the same time required a lot of autonomy and helped me step up my leadership skills.

According to Daniel Pink, intrinsic motivation emerges when people have autonomy over their task, time, technique, and team.[25] As people can decide what to work on, when to work, how to work, and who to work with, they are more intrinsically motivated to perform better. "Side project time" is a great example. Companies from 3M to Google, Atlassian, and many other companies have allowed or are allowing employees to work on side projects that are not about their main job for a certain percentage of work hours.[26] By letting people have a certain level of autonomy, they could expect better engagement in their work.

For me, better performance and well-regarded leadership resulted in two promotions in a row, even though I didn't try to get promoted. Experiencing this power of autonomy was another great gift of the Placeholder.

3. PURPOSE

One of my experiments during the Placeholder was to try something new to solve organizational problems. At Meta, teams were reorganized frequently. It meant multiple teams would merge or one team might break into multiple teams. Sometimes, teams would be dismantled or new teams created to meet various needs of business at different times. When my team merged with a different team, I was curious about how to bring two different team members together to make them more cohesive. It required building trust over time.

What would be essential in building trust as the first step? It definitely helps to know each other better. While social gatherings like team dinners are generally a good idea, expecting to learn more about multifaceted aspects of one another simply over team dinners was hard. *How about everyone sharing their side projects or hobbies they are passionate about with the rest of the team?*

I shared this idea with the team members and asked them to present it during the next team off-site. Frankly, I was apprehensive if people didn't even bother to prepare or they might grumble about "one more thing to do" on top of their packed schedules. It turned out my anxiety was baseless.

Everyone was so animated and excited to share what they personally cared about. Some showed their artwork such as photography and crafting, in which they were seriously investing time and effort outside work. Some talked about their volunteering activities they had been doing for communities for a long time. Some people even presented their secret recipes in a quick cooking session. Whatever it was, everyone enjoyed sharing what they found meaningful with their teammates and seeing one another as a whole person beyond their job titles or roles.

This quickly became a ground upon which trust could be built. As a result, it led to increasing the psychological safety and the sense of connection within my team. As they learned other sides of their coworkers, they were more patient with one another in conflicts and tried to find a better way to collaborate.

The level of trust and cohesion in my team was palpable, as shown in the biannual company-wide employee engagement survey. My team scored highest in the entire department. This experience made what mattered to me crystal clear and gave me a sense of purpose. My purpose was helping people and workplaces build a culture of well-being so both people and businesses could grow together sustainably.

What helped my team wasn't only better goal setting or more compensation but was about seeing one another as a whole person and being seen in such a way. I started dreaming of making that happen systematically. This experience fueled my purpose to train and coach people as well as teams to be more emotionally intelligent and compassionate at work.

These experiences of mastery, autonomy, and purpose in the Placeholder centered me with intrinsic motivation, which became an engine that propelled me further to craft, create, shape, and develop meaningful work for myself. This, I strongly believe, is the most valuable gift I got from the Placeholder.

INTRINSIC MOTIVATION IN THE PLACEHOLDER
Why is motivation 3.0 a big asset for our career and life? The answer lies in the changing landscape of work. The future requires us to be more driven by intrinsic motivation, because the type of work for humans is changing fast from algorithmic to heuristic tasks.[27]

An algorithmic task is a simple one where you follow a set of instructions to complete. Like computer code, an algorithmic task has a certain rule—"algorithm"—to follow to carry out a task, and it can be scripted. Algorithmic work usually involves transactional interactions. Cashiers at the department store and rideshare drivers are both algorithmic. The details of the job can be manualized, and anybody can do it as long as they follow the manual. Cashiers and drivers get paid for doing the job, over and over.

A heuristic task is the opposite. Codifying such tasks is hard; hence, it cannot be scripted. A heuristic task is more complex with many unexpected factors and nuanced contexts. Heuristic work involves tacit interactions and a high level of emotional intelligence. For example, coaching an executive who wants to reinvent themselves in a challenging time, pioneering a new category of industry, and creating a new virtual reality game are all heuristic. You have to test various options and create a new solution based on your experience and intuition every time.

Humans won't need to work on repetitive and routine algorithmic tasks for much longer because they will be automated or replaced by machines, robotics, and artificial intelligence. Instead, humans will be requested to work on more complex and creative heuristic tasks. This change is not a recent phenomenon with the widespread usage of generative artificial intelligence tools, such as ChatGPT, but has been already happening in the landscape of work. According to the US Bureau of Labor Statistics, between 1998 and 2004, only 30 percent of job growth came from algorithmic work, while 70 percent came from heuristic work in the US. Companies have already been streamlining and automating algorithmic work.[28]

This can sound like a crisis for humanity, but it isn't. We get to free ourselves from repetitive and mind-numbing tasks we find meaningless and work on more heuristic tasks that require creativity and in-depth insights from our own experiences.

Research by Teresa Amabile of Harvard Business School finds that intrinsic motivation is closely correlated with creativity, while extrinsic motivation undermines it.[29] This means we need to rely on our intrinsic motivation for heuristic tasks, such as creating a new category of product that no one knew they needed or solving problems that didn't exist before.

As you reflect, ideate, and experiment in the Placeholder, you become competent in driving your career with your own intrinsic motivations.

That'll become a huge asset to keep reinventing yourself, regardless of what happens externally. In the era of increasing heuristic work, we need to be more self-driven with intrinsic motivations. Working with extrinsic motivation based on reward and punishment will only make us obsolete.

THE RIPPLE EFFECT OF THE PLACEHOLDER INSIDE ORGANIZATIONS

With intrinsic motivation, you can acquire the ability to create uniquely meaningful work for yourself in the era of artificial intelligence. Beyond this, I strongly believe we can also address a lot of workplace issues from low engagement to burnout by adopting intrinsic motivation systemically inside organizations.

Abraham Maslow created humanistic psychology in the 1950s, denying the motivation 2.0 belief that human behavior was purely seeking reward and avoiding punishments like lab rats.[30] Furthermore, in the 1960s, Douglas McGregor, MIT management professor, challenged the assumption of Adam Smith that humans are basically "lazy" so we wouldn't do much without external rewards and punishments. He claimed people have higher drives, which can benefit businesses if their managers and leaders acknowledge and embrace such innate drives.[31]

In 2000, Richard Ryan and Edward Deci created the "Self-Determination Theory." With this theory, they argued that we have three innate psychological needs: competence, autonomy, and relatedness. When those needs are met, we are motivated, productive, and feel a true sense of well-being.[32]

In human nature is where we want to grow through mastery, engage with autonomy, and pursue meaning through purpose and relatedness, as many researchers suggested since the mid-twentieth century.

Despite this, our workplace systems having not evolved to reflect it at all is strange. Instead, organizations have designed systems and operated based on extrinsic motivation—from the compensation model to job assignment, performance evaluation, etc. This explains why more than three quarters of people at work don't feel engaged.

Stories of mine and people I interviewed in this book are testaments to how the Placeholder enables us to work with stronger intrinsic motivation. The autonomy, mastery, and purpose they experienced in the Placeholder experiments helped them deeply engage at work. For any organizations that want to improve job satisfaction, teamwork, and engagement among employees, offering systemic support for people to wander and explore different ideas for their careers is worth it.

This might sound counterintuitive to business leaders. They could ask, "What do you mean by allowing them to pursue something completely different from their job? I am not paying for that!" Such a reaction is understandable, but let us remember once again the world is changing and we need to adopt a new operating model of inspiration if we want to engage people deeply and create sustainable businesses together.

If we don't consider this new operating model, we might exacerbate many symptoms of the current workplace problems such as disengagement, loneliness, stress, and burnout. Essentially, these symptoms resulted from the clash between two different motivation models—the extrinsic motivation our workplaces have been operating from and the intrinsic motivation people inside organizations want now.

Perhaps now is the time for us as a society to enter the Placeholder collectively and experiment with this new operating model to see how the innate human desire for intrinsic motivation could help us engage in our work better with a sense of well-being. In the true spirit of the Placeholder, we can experiment, learn insights, and improve the system and culture of workplaces to thrive with deep engagement at work and the sense of well-being. Everyone does something meaningful for themselves, and the business grows as a result.

*****

As we explored in this chapter, the stakes are high if we do not become truly career-elastic based on what matters to us. Working with a sense of well-being, which will in turn benefit workplaces with deeper engagement, is critical for us individually. Furthermore, working with a sense of well-being is not only an ideal but a new imperative for organizations in the future of work at a society level.

The Placeholder is a potent place for us to not only create meaningful work for ourselves but also cultivate the capacity to change without difficulty. Now it's time to explore what the Placeholder is all about and how to apply it to ourselves.

PART 2

Image by Miroo Kim

CHAPTER 3

Welcome to the Placeholder!

What marks the beginning of the Placeholder? It may vary depending on people, but a couple of common signals exist. If you continue to suffer from a sense of emptiness and meaninglessness at work no matter what you try, you might be verging on the Placeholder. Or if you discover yourself asking more fundamental questions of "Why?" rather than "What?" or "How?", it's likely that the Placeholder is waving at you to join.

What does the Placeholder look like? What happens in the Placeholder? Here's a sneak preview of the Placeholder through Katie's journey.

KATIE'S PLACEHOLDER: APPLYING THREE PERSPECTIVES TO A WICKED PROBLEM

"Why do I want this so much?" One day, Katie asked herself this question out of frustration. She had been working hard at a prestigious nonprofit consulting firm for nine years since the business school. She was passionate about building nonprofit strategies for various clients, and she excelled in her job. Katie became a revered leader by the team she led and a seasoned executive skillfully managing the client relationships.

Yet, she didn't get due recognition from her firm—the big promotion she had wanted for so long and deserved with her hard work. She did everything she could do, ticking all the boxes. She was respected by her peers, management, and clients and put extra hours and effort into work. But it still didn't happen.

While pushing harder and harder to get what she wanted impetuously, she started probing into why she wanted the promotion fundamentally. *Why is promotion so important?* She reasoned, "Because I want to be recognized for my good performance. Because I deserve to progress to the senior level in the firm like my peers." *Okay, but why does that matter so much to me? Do I really want it, like more than anything else?* Katie couldn't answer this definitively. She wanted to ponder over it more.

In retrospect, asking this series of "why" questions was momentous for Katie, which marked the beginning of her Placeholder. To understand why it mattered to climb up the ladder in her firm, it wasn't enough to think about it by herself. She had to do something about it, but she didn't know exactly what to do or where to start. This wasn't familiar to her as other common career questions like "What should I do to get promoted?" or "How can I get a XYZ job at ABC company?" Asking herself "Why do I want this so much?" challenged her to go to a completely new place she hadn't been before.

Think about the last time you were figuring out how to go to a new location for the first time. The place is completely unknown to you. What do you do first? You search it up on a Google map or any other maps of your choice. With a single tab, the map shows the distance, the fastest route, and the estimated time it would take to get there. Wouldn't it be so nice to have such a tool for the Placeholder? Unfortunately, it doesn't exist. Even if it existed, it would be useless because you don't even know where you are trying to go.

Although no map exists for the Placeholder and what happens in it differs depending on people, a helpful framework applies to all the Placeholder experiences, which looks a lot like design thinking.

Design thinking is a nonlinear and iterative process, commonly used by designers or product managers. Design thinking is also known as the prescription for innovating products and services within business and social contexts because it is highly effective to tackle ill-defined or unknown challenges, also known as "wicked problems."[1] These types of troubles are the ones we face at the beginning of the Placeholder, making us feel stuck. They demand us to ideate unconventionally, take actions immediately, and constantly iterate.

Encountering her own wicked problem, Katie learned how to apply three unique perspectives of the Placeholder.

PERSPECTIVE 1: BE LIKE AN ANTHROPOLOGIST TO LEARN ABOUT YOURSELF

The design thinking process starts with research to gain an empathic understanding of the users and defines the core problems from users' perspective.[2] Likewise, in the beginning of the Placeholder, you are called to empathize with yourself and define the real problems that become the foundation of creating the work you want to do.

In the Placeholder, the user and the researcher are the same person: *you*. You need to pay close attention to your needs and wants by approaching yourself like an anthropologist, in a curious, objective, and empathetic perspective. You get to deeply understand your behaviors, motivations, and inner world. It involves stepping back from your usual self-narratives and exploring your life as if you are an observer studying a culture—in this case, *your own personal culture*—as an anthropologist would do.

By asking herself questions such as "Why do I want this so much?" and "Why does this matter to me? Or does it?" and "Why is this so distressing to me that I didn't get promoted at the same time as my peers?" Katie attempted to understand her deepest needs.

"It's easier to see in retrospect than at the time, but I had to pay attention to many signals," Katie recalled in an interview with me. "I was probably burned out and didn't see it at the time. I remember losing a lot of hair in the shower, and that didn't feel normal, but I didn't think of it as a big deal." Her peers who got promoted faster seemed to be cruising and didn't struggle as much. That made her doubt that she might not have been a natural fit for the job. She also questioned, "Is this true? What does it mean, essentially?"

How it unfolded was jarring and uncomfortable, but it pushed her to understand her fundamental needs more deeply. Had everything happened in the way she wanted; she might have never questioned it. "I don't think I fully understood the implications of the question 'Why do I want this?' at the time," Katie reflected. She didn't get the answer right away. The process was a long one of letting go of ego and old assumptions over a couple of years.

Katie didn't shrug off these signals but delved into them. Like an anthropologist with curiosity and empathy, she asked a lot of her friends and coworkers about how they thought of their work and what they wanted to do. She started working with a professional coach to get different perspectives of what she wanted. She began dabbling in some activities that piqued her interest naturally, like yoga, and she signed up for a yoga instructor training. She had no serious intention to become a yoga teacher, but simply wanted to learn. Doing so was one of many attempts she took to empathize with her own needs.

Doing this, the first thing she could see clearly was what didn't matter to her anymore. She confided, "I kind of wanted to be able to update my LinkedIn page with my new title that I made to a partner of my firm. I wanted to be able to tell people I have this title, which is a little bit embarrassing in retrospect because who cares?" She had to accept she had identified herself with her accomplishments or titles.

"But that's not necessarily me. That's one way to define myself, but it did not bring the most fulfillment," she said with clarity.

Based on the insights she gathered about herself, Katie sensed that actually advancing her career at the firm might not be what mattered to her after all. Though still vague, that intuition led her to define her problem better. Upon her own self-reflection and conversation with others, she realized what she truly enjoyed was developing people both for herself and others.

Katie not only loved reading articles and books about self-development but was great in applying them into real cases of people, guiding them to develop themselves like a great coach. Many of her business school friends could attest to this because they were often the beneficiaries of her great informal coaching for various issues at work. She intuited she was leaning in a certain direction.

Being her own anthropologist, Katie understood her underlying needs more in-depth and saw clearly that the motivation behind her needs to get promoted in the firm was extrinsic, not intrinsic. This helped her clarify what truly motivated her intrinsically—developing people. She was able to define her problem with clarity, from the question of *What should I do to get promoted and be recognized by others?* to *How might I find a way to work with others to help them develop themselves?*

PERSPECTIVE 2: BE LIKE A DESIGNER TO IDEATE, IDEATE, AND IDEATE

Another important stage in the design thinking process is to create ideas by challenging common assumptions. At the end of this stage, you get to choose the best ideas to move forward with prototyping and testing.[3]

Ideation is an important element in the Placeholder as well. After you glean the insight about yourself like an anthropologist, you take the perspective of a designer now, creating all the ideas from mundane to outrageous. No bad idea exists and no limit applies. By testing them quickly, you can narrow down to a couple of ideas that you'd like to experiment more deeply.

But unlike in design thinking, ideation in the Placeholder happens in a much more fluid and organic way because the "product" of the Placeholder is your work—an inseparable part of your life. It's not a standalone product or service you can test in isolation. This makes it particularly challenging, as the limiting beliefs you've internalized throughout your career can often block you from generating truly new ideas for you.

However, with the clearly defined problem statement based on your own intrinsic needs, it's also hard *not* to challenge your limiting beliefs of what you can do. That's what Katie also did; she kept pushing the boundary of her ideas and envisioned them to support her true needs like a designer.

One of her early ideas was to move from a full-time position to a part-time position in her consulting firm to have more time and mental space to explore other options. Another idea was to shift her position from a client-facing role to managing career development for consultants internally. These moves were unconventional for her peers at the firm. They viewed it as a career-limiting move to go from an external client-facing consultant to an internal role. Plus, she was cutting down work hours by becoming a part-timer rather than pouring more hours and heart into work. As Katie kept ideating, she became a bit bolder, asking, "How about taking on a consulting client of my own?"

It would be a lie to say she was 100 percent confident with her ideas. She was conscious that her ideas were not conventional in consulting, but that was the point. Her problem statement was no longer about how to progress her career at her firm but about "How might I find a way to work with others to help them develop themselves?" Her new ideas had to be outside the boundary of what she was used to.

In order to do this, she had to have some time to explore other options; hence, a part-time position. She also wanted to try out what it's like to actively guide others to develop themselves; hence, taking the internal role to develop the careers of consultants. If she were serious about this problem statement, she would eventually have to leave the firm and need to start her own business; hence, independent consulting experience.

Regarding all these ideas she tried, she recalled, "Because what I was trying was counterintuitive to my peers, I remember feeling really worried about it at first. But at the same time, I was excited that it was naturally aligned with my interests."

In her ideation stage, all the ideas she came up with supported her problem statement, and she had no expectation for any specific outcomes. These ideas didn't spring up magically all at once. They came at different times over a few years, but they were pushing the existing boundary she had little by little every time.

This point is important. You don't need to go to the far-fetched idea first. As long as your ideas speak to your redefined problem statement, you can start small and build from there. What's important to remember is to not limit your ideas from the perspective of others or old assumptions about yourself. Anything counts.

PERSPECTIVE 3: BE LIKE A MAD SCIENTIST TO EXPERIMENT

In design thinking, out of ideas you created, you will produce a number of inexpensive prototypes quickly to investigate the key solutions to the problem. The prototypes are investigated and then accepted, improved, or rejected based on the user experience. Then you will verify the best solution identified from prototyping. However, the result from verification isn't necessarily the end product but rather is used to redefine further problems and to create even better solutions.[4]

The Placeholder is also a highly iterative process like this, and this third perspective is the most critical. You get to create a career uniquely meaningful to you by experimenting your best ideas like a mad scientist. Doing so is different from leaving your current job and applying for a new one, thinking that will be it. You keep testing all the ideas you came up with repeatedly and narrow down to a few prototypes you find intrinsically most motivating for you. Like in the design thinking process, the experiment in the Placeholder should be easy to do without much resources. The emphasis is on experimenting, not perfecting an experiment.

Katie learned enough of her natural strength as a people developer by testing a couple of ideas at her firm. She narrowed down a few ideas and finally left the firm to try them out further in a new environment. She joined a boutique nonprofit consulting firm as a senior executive hoping she could have more impact on developing others internally and externally.

At the same time, she went through a rigorous professional coach certificate training for a whole year and started practicing coaching. As she coached more people who wanted to become good leaders as the first-time executives, she started taking her executive coaching practice more seriously. This led to finally launching her own business, Onwards Coaching.

Is this the end result of her Placeholder? Not quite.

In the beginning of the Placeholder, Katie had no inkling of what she wanted to do next. She simply had a question. But it feels different to her now. "I have much more of a sense of what I enjoy doing, what I'm actually good at, and what matters to me. Now I have many more ideas for what I like to do about coaching first-time managers and C-level executives," she said. That's for now, but in the near future, she wants to experiment developing leaders more systematically.

As you can see, she has an increased level of understanding of what matters to her, which enables her to investigate and refine the type of executive coaching she'd like to experiment with more new ideas. She'll proceed with further iterations and make changes to her coaching like a mad scientist. In this reiterative loop, Katie will continue to gain new insights, develop new ways to coach her clients, and evolve her business to develop people further. In future iterations, it may shift to something that looks different from coaching too. Katie feels more relaxed and open with a perpetual state of flux, being clear of her needs and wants. "I have much more foresight and feel more directed," she said.

Six years passed from the time when Katie asked herself the question "Why do I want this so much?" about her promotion, to the moment of launching her own coaching business. Katie's mindset about her career changed fundamentally after trying these perspectives of an anthropologist, designer, and mad scientist in the Placeholder. She says, "Now my mindset has become like, 'Oh, just try it.' If it doesn't stick, you could do something else." All the experiments she did in the Placeholder so far reassured her about her decision to be where she is now. It may change in the future, but she knows she simply needs to try putting on the hats of an anthropologist, a designer, and a mad scientist again.

NOW, IT'S YOUR TURN

You might say, "Well, this is easier in retrospect. I get the importance of trying different things out to create the work I find truly meaningful and motivating, but it's not that simple or easy for me to do this. I have responsibilities to fulfill and have no mental space for trying things out like her!"

I hear you. I do. When I started my Placeholder, I hesitated with similar thoughts too. Although I wasn't married and didn't have children at that time, I had to support my aging parents financially and help out my siblings in need. Plus, I had a pretty demanding full-time job, which made me think in a binary way that I must quit it to even think about any changes in the first place. Obviously, that wasn't an option for me.

If you want to close the door to your current work because it doesn't serve you anymore and open a new door to the new career you find meaningful and intrinsically motivating, you need to go through a hallway. That's the Placeholder. You cannot magically leap from one door to another. Although that sounds pretty darn attractive, that is magical thinking.

The Placeholder is the hallway that can lead you to many more doors. After you try opening many other doors in the hallway, you get to eventually make your own door—one just for you. That's what I did. So did Katie and many others I interviewed in this book. We didn't do this because we didn't have to worry about the balance in our bank accounts, nor did we not have any qualms about leaving the career track we invested our time and effort in. We did it because we all knew we couldn't satiate our need for change in the old ways anymore. We didn't know what it would look like when we started our Placeholder, but we crafted, shaped, or created our career by understanding ourselves better, following new ideas and testing them.

One thing many people I interviewed for this book expressed was "I wish I knew I was going through the Placeholder because then I would have worried and doubted less about myself." I feel the same way. Had I known I was going through a phase of meaningful changes in which all I needed was to be attentive to myself, be open to new ideas, and put some of them to the test, it would have been so much less stressful.

In the next four chapters, my intention is to light up this hallway of the Placeholder as bright as possible for you and show what you can do to craft the door for yourself. You will see what it means to apply each perspective of an anthropologist, designer, and mad scientist to your Placeholder experience in more detail. You will also see stories of how others did it.

For your Placeholder, this book will light up your path with valuable perspectives you can apply to yourself as you read along. I'll also put a spotlight on what to be aware of in the Placeholder and unexpected gifts from it too. This hallway, after all, isn't so scary or impassable, with booby traps and pits. It's totally safe and could be fun too.

CHAPTER 4

The First Perspective: Be Like an Anthropologist to Learn about Yourself

Before you tell your life what you intend to do with it, listen for what it intends to do with you. Before you tell your life what truths and values you have decided to live up to, let your life tell you what truths you embody, what values you represent.

—PARKER J. PALMER

GREGORY UNCOVERS HIS SUPERPOWER IN THE PLACEHOLDER

Gregory Kim is an executive coach for startup founders. He's also advising startups for their businesses and products. Prior to this, he built quite an impressive résumé with great credentials and experiences. But Gregory says he was "stuck" in the rat race for a long time.

After college, he thought it would be a good idea to be an investment banker, so he worked hard for it. When he became a successful investment banker, he realized that wasn't what he wanted exactly. So he went to business school to figure that out. During business school, he learned about consulting and thought maybe he wanted to do that. He joined one of the top three consulting firms and worked as a consultant for three years, rising up as an excellent leader. But he realized that wasn't what he wanted either. What could it be? He left consulting to work in a startup in a leadership role, thinking he wanted to do that.

Disappointingly, it turned out that wasn't exactly what he *wanted* to do either.

He didn't think he wasted his time at the investment bank, consulting firm, and startup. Gregory certainly achieved a lot in each job and learned so much from all the experiences. Yet, Gregory wonders if he could have managed each transition of his work from a different perspective.

In the interview with me, he reflected, "In each transition from one job to another, I think I was getting burned out, as I took every job too seriously, as if each one was '*the* job' for me. Had I known I was in the Placeholder and I was just tinkering with different ideas, I wouldn't have burned myself out." Gregory suspected he projected what others valued most into his career rather than what mattered to him. He got more curious about how to identify what he *really* wanted to do, but not in a deductive way.

"After going through these multiple transitions, I started seeing a through line in every job I took—helping other people accomplish their goals that they thought impossible," Gregory said. Based on his observation, one of the biggest obstacles for people to win at work was their own limiting belief from a misguided self-reflection. In every job he did, he was always good at translating a blurry self-reflection of a person into a clear understanding and got them to see how to achieve their "win," whatever their goals might have been. This really mattered to him. The question shifted for him from "What do I want to do?" to "What matters to me?"

For Gregory, each job in investment banking, consulting, and at the startup was an experiment in his own Placeholder. They informed him of what mattered to him—playing the role of a *translator* for others so they could have higher clarity of self-awareness. He never thought he wanted to do this, but he knew clearly that it mattered to him. With this insight, Gregory has been constantly ideating and developing other experiments in iteration, such as coaching and advising startup founders and executives.

Gregory said, at first, gaining this insight of himself as the translator for other people's self-awareness hurt his confidence a little. "I didn't really know how to appreciate or value that quality of myself. It took me a long time to realize and appreciate this insight, and I am still learning how to embrace this *superpower* of mine and incorporate it into my work now." But he believes in this superpower. It is not only meaningful to him but a unique and valuable contribution to the world.

"It's clearly different from what I thought I wanted to do in the past. It's not a reflection of what other people desire in me at all," he said. The jury is still out on whether he can make a decent living to support his family with this work, but Gregory is deeply interested and willing to experiment further with this knowledge of what matters to him.

WHAT YOU WANT VERSUS WHAT MATTERS TO YOU
Let's do a quick thought exercise here. Try to answer the following questions in each case; mine are in italic.

Case 1
Q: Do you want ice cream from Salt & Straw (or any ice cream store in your neighborhood)?
A: *Of course!*

Q: Does it matter to you?
A: *No.*

Case 2

Q: Do you want to become a vice president or CEO?
A: *Yes.*
Q: Does it matter to you?
A: *Yes.*
Q: Why does it matter to you?
A: *Because all my friends are either vice presidents or C-levels.*
Q: Why does it matter to be like your friends?
A: *Hmm... actually, it doesn't really matter whether I am like my friends or not.*

Case 3

Q: Do you want to travel to Nova Scotia in Canada?
A: *Yes.*
Q: Does it matter to you?
A: *Absolutely.*
Q: Why does it matter to you?
A: *Because I really want to visit the Anne of Green Gables Museum on Prince Edward Island. Anne was my childhood hero who embodied all the qualities I found so important in living a good life.*

We want many things and experiences in our life, but when it comes to what matters, we often discover only a few things truly matter to us uniquely. I believe this is because what we want is highly conditioned by others and society, as shown in the "mimetic theory," created by French philosopher René Girard.[1]

According to him, we are creatures who don't know what to want, and we turn to others in order to make up our minds. Girard states that all desire is merely an imitation of another's, and we want them only because others have endowed values and meanings on a certain object.

This means our object or goal is only desired because of societal ideas and is not based on personal preference like most believe.[2]

You might ask, "Is it wrong to do what others want in my career?" It's not wrong, up to a certain degree. If you are beginning your career right out of college, you might look at what your friends do and follow where they are going. That's not a bad way to start. If you are lucky, you might be able to discover what truly matters to you that way too. However, the runway of following what others value tends to run short. If you start noticing yourself suffering from being hollow, drained, unfulfilled, and empty with your career as I did, it means you need a new benchmark. Perhaps it's time to look for not what you want but what matters to you.

You might also ask, "Isn't what matters to us also influenced by others?" That question is fair, but the answer is "Unlikely" because what matters to you is based on your self-awareness—what you know about yourself. Only *you* have lived *your* life and gone through *your* experiences at work. The same is true for me. Only I have lived *my* life and gone through *my* own career. Therefore, what matters to *me* would be different from what matters to someone else, even though they might have been to the same school or had the same career. Sure, we might share some common things, but our commonalities are never identical.

Discerning between what we want and what matters to us is critical. "What do I want?" is the question rooted in personal preferences or immediate gratification. It can make us disproportionately focus on individualistic or material goals such as wealth, comfort, or status. This question also reflects temporary or surface-level ambitions, often shaped by external influences like societal expectations or trends, as indicated by the mimetic theory.[3] Moreover, our wants are fluid and may shift based on circumstances or emotions.

"What matters to us?" challenges us to uncover the enduring principles, values, and beliefs that guide our lives. This question helps us see something larger than our individual self, such as relationships with others, contributions to communities, or living authentically according to our values. In essence, this question guides us to focus on what gives our life *meaning* and brings the lasting sense of fulfillment as a result.

The meaning of our life is not something we can copy from others but unique to each of us. Viktor Frankl, the great psychologist and Holocaust survivor, spoke of this in his book *Man's Search for Meaning*.

> Questions about the meaning of life can never be answered by sweeping statements. "Life" does not mean something vague, but something very real and concrete, just as life's tasks are also very real and concrete. They form a man's destiny, which is different and unique for each individual. No man and no destiny can be compared with any other man or any other destiny. No situation repeats itself, and each situation calls for a different response.[4]

This perspective is the first one you try in the Placeholder by shifting the old question of *wanting* to the new question of *mattering* and *meaning*.

"What should I do for my work?" ⟶ "What matters to me for my work?"
Old Question   The Placeholder Question

Image by Miroo Kim

BECOMING OUR OWN ANTHROPOLOGISTS

To discover what matters and what is meaningful to us, we need to take the perspective of anthropologists for ourselves. Why anthropologists? A couple of characteristics in the way they work can be highly effective for us to discover what matters to us in the Placeholder.

First, anthropologists see everything holistically. They consider all aspects of human life—biological, cultural, historical, and social—in an integrated way. They look at the big picture to understand how different factors influence human behavior and culture.[5] For Gregory, every job experience in the past, his reflection on who and what influenced him in his life, and his awareness of ongoing discomfort in every job transition became important data for him. They helped him realize the through line of all—being a translator of self-awareness for others—and that mattered to him.

Second, anthropologists like to observe in complete immersion. They immerse themselves in the communities they study, sometimes for months or years, to gain a deep understanding of their way of life. The cornerstone of their research method is to engage in daily activities of participants while observing.[6] When I was trying to discover what mattered to me, I couldn't expect it to emerge miraculously like in a eureka moment. Beyond contemplating my past experiences, I had to talk to people who knew me well and also expose myself to many new experiences, such as taking classes and joining new communities. Some experiments helped me learn what mattered more to me, while others weren't so useful. Being absorbed in these experiences, I could have better clarity of what was meaningful to me.

Third, anthropologists often use the method of longitudinal research. They conduct long-term studies, observing changes and developments in communities over time. This allows them to capture dynamic processes and shifts in cultures and societies.[7] For both Gregory and me, it took at least a couple of years to discover what mattered to us. We both observed how we changed over time internally and externally. Discovering what matters to us takes time, so thinking of this process as the longitudinal research of anthropologists is helpful.

✪ GUIDE: HOW TO DISCOVER WHAT MATTERS TO YOU LIKE AN ANTHROPOLOGIST

Now, you might be wondering how to become an anthropologist for yourself to discover what matters to you in your career. The good news is you already have a lot of data points you could harvest insights from—your own experiences so far. As was the case for Gregory and me, your relationship with people and past work experiences can be a rich field of information from your own anthropologist perspective.

In the following exercises, you can learn how to extract insights on what matters to you by reflecting on your career and life so far holistically. Remember, these are just ideas to kick-start an anthropologist perspective for your Placeholder; once you get used to it, you will be able to see every part of your experience in such a viewpoint easily.

EXERCISE 1: UNDERSTANDING YOUR VALUE THROUGH PEOPLE YOU ADMIRE

Marcus Aurelius opens the beginning of his famous *Meditations* with a list of people in his life and their qualities he admired. Starting from his grandfathers, to parents, tutors, friends, historical figures, and gods, the qualities he admired from them filled the entire Book 1.[8]

Why did he start *Meditations* with the people and their qualities he admired? Because they carried important values for him. Values are qualities or traits you find important in life and want to live by.

They work like great signposts or solid guardrails that direct to what matters to you. However, you might not be able to answer easily if I simply ask, "What are your values?" Typical qualities that most people find important—such as love, courage, respect, relationship, etc.—may come up in your mind, but it can stay abstract and impersonal. This value exercise is effective as it helps you identify your values much more easily and concretely.

Each step is timed in parentheses. Please try to not spend more time on each step of the exercise, to let your intuition play.

Image by Miroo Kim

Step 1. Identify three to five people in your life you admire and deeply respect. You want to emulate them or what they did in your life and work. They are not necessarily people who you love or like, but you admire them because of what they did or what they stand for (five minutes).

- It could be someone you know personally or a public figure you don't know in person.

- It could be a real person or a fictional character from a movie, book, or game.
- It could be someone who's no longer with us.

Step 2. Write down their names, the traits or qualities you admire about them, and any circumstances or contexts when they showed such traits or qualities (fifteen minutes).

Step 3. As you review what you wrote, identify three to five qualities or traits that stand out to you as core values (five minutes).

- Notice how it feels to see the list of core values. Do you resonate with it? Are you surprised to see some values that you never thought of?

Step 4. Reflect if those values are present or not in your current work (five minutes).

- If they are present, list examples of how such values are manifesting in your work. The more detailed, the better.
- If the core values are not really present in your work, first note that it's okay and normal. Now think about what stops you from manifesting such values in your work. What are some small steps you can take to have your core values present in your work?

EXERCISE 2: OUTSIDE-IN REFLECTIONS

Sometimes, regardless of what we do for work, we are already showing what matters to us in our behavior and action. But more often than not, we are not "aware" that we are doing it. At this point is when we need to get some help from others about their reflections on us. This exercise guides you to reflect on your values through the eyes of others.

As this exercise requires you to take feedback from others, give it a week or so to complete the exercise.

Step 1. Think of five to ten people from your life who know you well—friends, colleagues, ex-colleagues, mentors, etc. You want a mix of people who have seen you in different contexts and handling different situations.

Step 2. Send them an email or text asking them for a favor. This will probably take them about twenty to thirty minutes, so be willing to return the favor in any way you can in the future and mention it in your email. Also, give them three to five days to reply. You will ask the following sets of questions in the email.

- *Write the stories of times when I was at my best from your view with the following three points.*
  - *What was I doing?*
  - *How did you know I was at my best?*
  - *What surprised or impressed you most about how I handled the situation?*
- *Please answer these questions:*
  - *When in need, what would you like to seek my advice about?*
  - *If you were to explain about me to someone else, what would you say?*
  - *From your perspective, what's one thing I don't appreciate about myself but should?*

Step 3. As you receive each reflection and read it, circle or underline the parts that resonate with you. Notice if any common threads show up across all reflections from others. Also, don't forget to send them a thank-you email.

- If you have done Exercise 1 already, compare the result of this exercise with your reflection from Exercise 1 and see what comes up.

POST-EXERCISES: PAUSE AND REFLECT

After doing these exercises, you can reflect on the following questions, either thinking about it, journaling your thoughts, or having a conversation about it with someone you'd like as a thought partner.

- How do you feel as you read through your values through people you admire and reflections from other people in your life?
- What did you discover about yourself that you weren't aware of before?
- Is there anything surprising to you? What is it, and why is it surprising?
- Reflect on the results of two exercises above as if you are reviewing it from the perspective of a third party. Consider the following points:
    - Exercise 1 can uncover values (what you believe in).
    - Exercise 2 may reveal your unconscious actions or how you influenced other people, in which you embodied what mattered to you without being aware.
- Write down what matters to you. For example:
    - What matters to [Your Name] is_____

*****

In observing yourself like an anthropologist through these exercises, you will learn more deeply about values that matter to you (Exercise 1) and how others see you when you are at your best, subconsciously embodying your values (Exercise 2). Inevitably, these exercises will also reveal the discrepancy between what you are doing in your current career and what could deeply matter to you.

So, what shall you do with these insights? Now it's time to wear the new hat of a designer.

CHAPTER 5

The Second Perspective: Be Like a Designer to Ideate Yourself

Many doors might look like walls at first.
—MATTHEW BRENSILVER, MEDITATION TEACHER

AMIT'S INTERACTIVE VIRTUAL STUDIO
What is success? What would it look like to do this job in the future? These types of questions were constantly cycling through Amit's brain for a while, as he shared in the interview with me. Sometimes he couldn't sleep because it was bothering him so much, and it was actually impacting his personal life too. Amit would continue to think about this, half listening to his wife over dinner. He also got cynical and found himself complaining to other people about his work much more often than ever.

Amit worked in the finance department of a big tech firm. It had been a good career for him—interesting and innovative problems to solve, smart people to work with, and great compensation. Yet, internally, he started noticing conflicts. What used to matter to him—the brand name of the workplace, the big bold missions to change the world, and the financial reward that came with it—no longer did. He felt uneasy and somewhat lost, even. How would he measure the success of his career now? More fundamentally, what did he work for? These questions kicked off a whole series of personal investigations for Amit in many conversations. He was stepping into the Placeholder.

One of the influential books Amit read during this time was *Man's Search for Meaning* by Viktor Frankl, in which he documented his own experiences at a Nazi concentration camp during World War II. Viktor Frankl observed firsthand how crucial it was for him and other camp prisoners to be clearly aware of the meaning of their lives even in the utmost suffering.[1] Those prisoners who understood what they existed for could survive the horror of the Holocaust better than those who merely had hopes of survival.

This initiated Amit asking himself an instrumental question: *Which work is worth putting myself through so much stress, anxiety, and so on for?* The problem wasn't finding another job that could satisfy him but figuring out *what mattered to him.*

A more vigorous and winding process of investigation, conversations, and reflection went on over a couple of years from the perspective of an anthropologist. Through this process, Amit gained higher clarity on what mattered to him. He said, "Beyond the basic sustenance, I came down to three things that mattered to me: building meaningful relationships with other people, continuing to learn with a curious mind, and developing the ability to navigate any ups and downs at work, which are inevitable." He hadn't deliberately thought about these three things in the past, but now, he wanted to focus on shaping his work around these fundamentals.

Like a designer, he started searching for ideas aligned with these three principles. Per a suggestion by one of his friends, Amit started documenting all the insights he learned from working on those wide range of ideas. He named it "Amit's Reflections." What he wanted to check was how each idea would align with his three fundamental values.

Then he invited a group of close friends and previous coworkers he trusted—namely, his thought partners—to review his reflections and asked them to share their feedback and insights. Basically, this made the document a live virtual lab to evolve his ideas by sharing, vetting, questioning, clarifying, and expanding together with his thought partners. This ideation system helped Amit develop his ideas to align his future work with what mattered to him. Amit shared of this ideation process:

"A lot of the questions early in our career have much easier answers. You know, things like you want to go to business school or you want to go work at Google. You don't need that much crazy advice, and the decision process is pretty straightforward. But the type of questions I am thinking about now requires a totally different approach. For me, going to a bunch of people to figure out new ideas and have conversations to help me vet them is important. Then I test ideas. Once I write things down, having someone to run through my ideas is great for me."

Running many ideas through this interactive lab, Amit came down with a couple of ideas that were worth experimenting. One of these short-listed ideas was to start an indoor pickleball court. When he moved to Pittsburgh, he got really into playing pickleball and loved it. Being new to the city with no friends or acquaintances, he truly appreciated pickleball as a "social fitness" that enabled him to meet new people so easily and connect with them authentically.

On the court, it didn't matter what your profession, race, age, or social status was. He played with people from all walks of life—a retiree to a professor, an electrician, a karate studio owner, a librarian, etc. People were able to connect with one another simply by throwing their bodies around. Plus, it was a great workout. But one problem was most pickleball courts were outdoors and it was deadly cold in Pittsburgh in the winter. Amit didn't want his newfound community to pause playing because of severe weather, so he started thinking about how to play pickleball indoors.

This project mattered to him because it was about building meaningful relationships—one of his principles to work for. The more he thought about it, the more he got excited about this idea. He started sharing his idea with some of the new pickleball partners he met. Through conversation with them, he learned perhaps he could try a pop-up event for an indoor pickleball first, which wouldn't require significant resources.

Through his pickleball connection, he met some other people who were running nonprofits in the community who could help him out to offer this as a community service. A karate studio master offered his help about how to run a fitness initiative like this. Amit needed to solve many problems, such as finding a free or low-cost indoor space for pop-up. Although Amit had never attempted to work on things like this before, he was willing to bootstrap and develop his ideas one by one with an open mind.

This experience completely changed how Amit saw his career. He said, "If I can professionally find a role aligned with my values—building positive and meaningful relationships, instilling a love of learning, or helping other people get past setbacks—that would be fantastic. I am trying this indoor pickleball idea, and I might fail with this, but the experience of pursuing something aligned with what truly matters to me is worth it. This is a win for me now."

IDEATE LIKE A CREATIVE DESIGNER

Creativity is not a talent. It is a way of operating.
—JOHN CLEESE, ACTOR AND COMEDIAN

If you have identified what matters to you, you are ready to ideate. But how? You might think, *I am not creative enough to generate so many ideas.* It could feel like facing a big wall, not knowing what to do with a pretty important insight about what truly matters to you. This sense of paralysis could happen because of our misunderstanding about creativity.

What kind of images come to your mind when you think of "creativity"? A wretched painter finally getting an inspiration for a masterpiece after agonizing for years? A mad scientist suddenly having an enlightening moment and discovering a revolutionary solution for humanity? This view on creativity was common until the mid-twentieth century; creativity was considered inexplicable and nebulous. Since then, many scientists and psychologists have discovered that creativity is not an inherent quality but a way of operating, which we can practice in our daily life, as John Cleese mentioned in his famous lecture in 1991.

Creativity is not a talent or ability we either have or not, according to John Cleese,[2] based on the seminal research in 1959 by Dr. Donald MacKinnon at UC Berkeley. In the research, MacKinnon and his colleagues concluded that the creative people had "simply acquired a facility for getting themselves into a particular mood—'a way of operating'—which allowed their creativity to function."[3]

So how can we develop this *way of operating* to be creative? Developing creativity is about choosing open versus closed mode, Cleese said.[4] He pointed out that closed mode was how we are most of the time when at work. We have a lot on our mind; so many tasks to complete with competing priorities in a tight schedule. The closed mode is an active and a slightly anxious mode in which we're a little impatient with ourselves, others, or both. Tension is in the closed mode and not so much humor.[5] Creativity is not possible in this closed mode.

By contrast, the open mode is relaxed, expansive, and perhaps less purposeful. We become more contemplative, more inclined to humor, and more playful as a result. In this mode, we are more curious, as we're not fixated on finding the right answer or solution quickly. As a result, we can play and welcome any ideas to float to the surface.[6]

In the Placeholder, operating in the open mode—generating ideas as freely as possible and challenging old assumptions—is critical to uncovering what we find truly meaningful. This approach is similar to the ideation process in design thinking, which is all about creating as many ideas as possible and narrowing down to the best ideas to move forward with prototyping and further experiments. In the perspective of a designer, we are now ideating as many potential inputs as possible for our Placeholder.

We make two common mistakes with ideation in the Placeholder. First, we may think we need to come up with radical ideas only from the get-go. Second, we may shun certain ideas from even considering based on habitual patterns or old assumptions. For example, as I was getting more interested in organizational culture, I thought perhaps I should quit my job and go get a PhD in organizational development first to start a new career for it. The idea was drastic but also overwhelming as it involved big decisions. The idea was also based on my old assumptions of how to make a change in career. "First, prove yourself with the most prestigious credentials."

Making such mistakes is understandable, but this is exactly why we need to operate in the *open* mode. We can start from familiar and mundane ideas and move to more unusual and bold ones. We get to develop bigger ideas by trying small ones constantly too. Instead of quitting my job and pursuing academic degrees, I got certified to teach an emotional intelligence course called Search Inside Yourself and started facilitating it for teams at Meta. When I met some other like-minded folks, I started running a community to practice mindfulness at work. A collection of every small idea that was easy to do led me to bigger, bolder, and more unconventional ones.

Basically, we don't need a specific talent to generate creative ideas for our Placeholder. We just need to remember to operate in an open mode like a designer. We have nothing to get stressed out about. In fact, you most likely already have some ideas you want to start with. You just need to warm up your mind a little to let them emerge. The following practices will help you warm up and kick-start your ideation before you know it.

✪ GUIDE: HOW TO IDEATE LIKE A DESIGNER

1. MINDSET—WHAT IF? WHY NOT? COULD IT BE?

To ideate, we need to first become comfortable with divergent thinking. As you ideate, the first rule is to *not* approach this as a problem to solve but something to play with. Graham Wallas, the English social psychologist and London School of Economics cofounder, would advise the same. Wallas was fascinated by how people came up with great ideas in history and conducted extensive research of various professions—from scientists and academics to artists, musicians, and businesspeople. Based on this, he wrote an insightful theory about the four stages of the creative process in the book, *The Art of Thought*, in 1926.

In this book, Wallas outlined four stages on how great ideas were born: preparation, incubation, illumination, and verification.[7]

- **Preparation:** Investigate the topic in all directions by accumulating intellectual resources out of which to construct new ideas. Preparation is when you sit down, focus, and do the deep work.

- **Incubation:** Allow your conscious mind to rest and let your subconscious mind step in to make loose associations between different concepts and experiences.
- **Illumination:** Illumination is a moment of sudden inspiration or revelation of ideas that have been cooking in the incubation phase. It's the "aha" or "eureka" moment.
- **Verification:** Verification is a time for more deep work to verify if the brilliant idea is actually applicable. The purpose is to test the validity of the idea and keep refining it.

When you try to come up with new ideas, you might focus on the illumination stage only when ideas pop up. However, for the illumination stage to happen, you would need to prepare with deep work as the ground for ideas ("preparation"). And most importantly, we must let the seeds of ideas take roots and sprout through the "incubation" stage.

The most counterintuitive point in Wallas's discovery was this incubation stage, when most creative thinkers such as Darwin or Beethoven in history let go of the need to "solve the problem" and just *relaxed* to incubate ideas. In other words, they didn't force themselves by doubling down their effort to ideate. This will only activate your convergent thinking, not divergent.

You have acquired valuable insights about what truly matters to you by observing yourself like an anthropologist. As you try to create new ideas based upon these self-insights, you might be tempted to approach it as a problem to solve. However, it is not a problem to solve but a *possibility to explore*. When you approach it as a problem to solve, you are doing convergent thinking—drilling down with hyper focus. If you approach it as possibilities to explore, you are doing divergent thinking—ideating with big pictures.

This mindset was critical in the case of Amit too. In his spreadsheet of a live virtual studio, he listed all kinds of ideas from "working with kids" to "running a retail store," "being a therapist," "working in a city government," "consulting," and "doing a pickleball pop-up," etc. As you can see, it's pretty divergent—a wide range of ideas. To cultivate this mindset, the most helpful questions to ask yourself are the following:

- **What if?** What if I do X, Y, or Z?
- **Why not?** Why not this? Why not that?
- **Could it be…?** Could it be A? Could it be B?

The amazing children's book writer Kate DiCamillo asked these questions through the character Leo Matienne in her book *Magician's Elephant*.[8] The book is a wonderful refrain for a positive mindset for children. But they are equally effective for you in this designer's perspective for the Placeholder. These questions help you counter the convergent tendency that makes you prune ideas too quickly as you branch out with many ideas. Amit was asking himself this too. What if I work with kids? Why not be a therapist? Could running an indoor pickleball court be meaningful?

In the world of chess, what distinguishes the great chess players from others is that they explore all ideas, even though some of them might look outrageous, bad, or risky at first. A lot of ideas don't make sense at first, but you can still explore them without pruning them too quickly. So resist your unwillingness to look at the seemingly odd, outrageous, or impossible ideas with these questions as you ideate. Many ideas that might have looked like walls will start emerging as doors for you.

2. ACTION—ENVISION AND EXPLORE

After I discovered what mattered to me, I felt stuck again. It felt like my creative mind froze all of a sudden. In retrospect, I clearly did not have the right mindset mentioned above. In case you have similar difficulties in ideating as I did, I would like to introduce you to two exercises that helped me unblock the channel for ideation and got me in the open mode like a designer. These exercises are also some of my clients' favorites. Let's explore each and you can give one or both a try.

Image by Miroo Kim

EXERCISE 1: ENVISION YOUR BEST POSSIBLE FUTURE

Envisioning helps you so much when ideating. Envisioning is about visualizing your best possible future. In making this future happen, you will have no constraints, and it'll exceed your expectations in every possible way. Sounds impossible? Well, the point of this exercise is not to evaluate its feasibility but get your mind to become as open and divergent as possible. Planning to make your future happen is not the point. Just imagine your best possible future is happening right now.

You can do this in two ways.

1) Version 1: Journaling: Write your response to the following prompt.

Prompt: What are you working on in five years if everything in your work life starting today exceeds your wildest expectations and reflects your most important values?

- Write as if you are writing a scene from a movie; be as descriptive as possible. Where are you? Who are you with? What are you doing? How are you feeling? What are you thinking?
- Write in the present tense as if it's happening now: "I am/do…" instead of "I will…"

2) Version 2: Using Generative AI tools (for example, ChatGPT, Claude, Gemini, Copilot, or any other AI tool of your choice): Do you have a strong inner critic that keeps interrupting in your creative flow, saying, "It won't be possible because of XYZ"? If so, this version could be helpful, because you are getting the help from the Gen AI tool that won't sabotage your creativity. Gen AI tools will envision for you based on inputs you write below, without getting interrupted by your inner critic.

Write your inputs to the following prompt, copy and paste the entire prompt, including your inputs into your favorite Gen AI tool. Ask it to share different versions for variations if you want to tweak some parts. See what you resonate with the best. Like Version 1, please write in the present tense as if it's happening now: "I am/do…" instead of "I will…"

Prompt:

"Everything in my career, starting from today, meets or exceeds my most optimistic expectations. I am invited to do a TED Talk and will discuss my work and my journey." Write a TED speech including the following information:

- Person: (Your name)
- Today's date: (Five years from today)
- Where I am now: (TED conference in Vancouver)
- What I am doing now: (What you wish to do in five years)
- What I am feeling right now: (How you imagine you feel in five years from today)
- Who is with me right now: (Important people you imagine to be with you five years from today)
- What matters to me now: (What matters to you)

EXERCISE 2: WRITING MULTIPLE PLACEHOLDER SCENARIOS

In this exercise, you imagine and write up many different versions of the next five years of your life. This exercise is inspired by the Odyssey Plans from the Designing Your Life workshop, created by Bill Burnett and Dave Evans, at Stanford d.school.[9] Burnett and Evans started calling them Odyssey Plans because each plan is an adventure, like the journey of Odysseus in the book written by Homer.[10]

Worth noticing is it has not only a single but multiple scenarios. The intention behind this approach is that creating multiple prototypes—like multiple Odyssey Plans—in parallel leads to more divergence, better design results, and increased self-efficacy, according to the research by the Stanford Graduate School of Education.[11] In other words, if you start with multiple ideas in parallel, you stay more open-minded and expand the boundaries of your ideas.

If you feel stuck with ideation at this point in your Placeholder, you can use this exercise to let your imagination loose about your future work scenarios, reflecting what matters to you in various ways. Here's the guidance for the Placeholder Scenarios.

Each scenario has times in parentheses. Please try to not spend more time on each step of the exercise in order to let your designer's perspective play.

Scenario 1: What are the easiest things you can do now right away that can bring you a little closer to what matters most to you? What is it like in five years? (twenty minutes)
Pick the easiest thing you can do now that might bring you a step closer to what matters most to you. Although it might be mundane, it can be something you can do easily without much resistance or change. What is it? It might be taking the online course or having a coffee chat with the person who's already doing the work you want to do. Imagine you are trying all the "easy options" in year one.

Now, jump to creating year five based on the assumptions from year one. Where do you want to be? What are you doing in year five based on your actions in year one? Then go ahead and map out year two, three, and four while referencing both year one and year five. What will you do in each year to start year one to get to year five?

Scenario 2: What would you like to work on if money or status were not an issue? If you had no constraints whatsoever, what would you do? (twenty minutes)
This scenario is different from Scenario 1 in that you can do whatever you want to do to work on what matters most to you. Imagine you can take the boldest actions from year one right away. You won't need to worry about whether you'd make a decent living with it, what other people would think of you, or anything else. What would you do in year one? What does year five look like? What does the evolution of year two, three, and four look like?

Scenario 3: What would it be like if you were to do the most unlikely things for you? (twenty minutes)
This scenario is different from Scenario 1 and 2 in that you imagine the most unlikely actions you'd take in order to work

in full alignment with what matters to you. Think of it as a version of Scenario 2 amplified to the maximum. If you are introverted, imagine you are extremely extroverted in this scenario and think of all the ideas you'd take as an extroverted person. If you are analytical, imagine you become an artist who doesn't think analytically at all in this scenario. What would you do in year one? What does year five look like? What will you do in year two, three, and four?

If you feel awkward and get stuck a bit in the beginning as you do this exercise, it's understandable. So did I. But trust me, your mind will get stretched as you write your Placeholder scenarios. After all, it's like a scenario for a movie. Imagining the wildest scenario of your career costs nothing. Don't overthink it. Just do it.

In each Placeholder scenario, you are investigating different possibilities and learning different things about you and the world around you. Although you create each scenario with the assumption that you are working on things that matter to you, what you end up doing in year five can be different in each scenario.

Remember, the goal of this exercise is *not* to find the "answer" to your problem. However, writing each of these scenarios can strengthen your muscle for many creative paths you never dreamed of. You might mix some ideas from each scenario or create completely new ideas based on this exercise. Before you know it, you might be working on some ideas from this exercise in the next five years.

*****

What kind of ideas emerged? How do you feel about them? The purpose of both exercises is not to come up with the best ideas but to get familiar with what's possible through ideation, being like a designer. In the first envisioning exercise, you expand your mind as much as possible so you can see the future unbounded by any assumptions. In the second Placeholder scenario exercise, you try to be as divergent as possible by thinking of various possibilities. Being like a designer, you learn to stay open to all kinds of ideas and check which ones are more aligned with what matters to you. This process is interactive and iterative, as you saw in Amit's story. After doing the exercises above, some ideas might be more resonant than others to you.

Now, it's time to wear the hat of a mad scientist to experiment, experiment, and experiment.

CHAPTER 6

The Third Perspective: Be Like a Mad Scientist to Experiment with Ideas

Do you prefer films based on books or the original books themselves? I usually prefer original books to films in general, but I have two exceptions. The first is *The Curious Case of Benjamin Button* (2008), the movie based on F. Scott Fitzgerald's original short story with the same title.[1] Another exception is *The Secret Life of Walter Mitty* (2013), the film based on James Thurber's original short story from 1939.[2]

In the 1939 original story, James Thurber satirizes how Walter Mitty escapes to the hypermasculine fantasies of his secret life from his humdrum days. He remains largely static in reality, not doing anything beyond daydreaming. Walter Mitty's desire to try different things and adventures in life is palpable throughout his active daydreaming. Reading the book, I couldn't stop wondering how it could have been different had he tried something, as it ended with yet another daydream and no action.

The 2013 movie *The Secret Life of Walter Mitty*, played and directed by Ben Stiller, expands on the original story. Walter Mitty works at *Life* magazine, which is expected to publish the last print issue before it goes digital 100 percent. Like in the original story, Mitty's life is monotonous and dull. As a negative asset manager of all the photography films for *Life*, his job is about to become extinct in the new era of digital media. He daydreams a lot about different lives he admired but assumed unreachable for himself.[3]

For example, he dreams of becoming those daring photographers who captured incredible moments in the wild for the magazine, even risking their lives. But in reality, he cannot even sign up for an online dating service because he couldn't fill out the "Been There" and "Done That" sections of his dating profile. Up to this point, it feels quite similar to the original story, but the 2013 movie takes quite a creative spin into a very different direction from the original. When Mitty has to find the missing negative for the magazine's final cover, he embarks on the unexpected adventures for it.[4] His daydreams come to life, and Walter Mitty undergoes significant self-transformation as a result.

The biggest difference between these two versions of *The Secret Life of Walter Mitty* is the actions Walter Mitty takes based on his daydreams in the film. In one scene of the movie, Mitty imagines the photographer waves to him to join his adventure. Dramatically, as it should be for a movie, Mitty walks out the door from his office without hesitation and flies straight to Greenland, where his first adventure begins.

For the rest of the film, no more division is present between his daydreams and reality. Daydreams become reality, and reality embodies daydreams. Many things go wrong and way too many unexpected things happen against his expectation, but he tries them all. When he comes back to his seemingly uneventful life again from his adventures, he is no longer the same Walter Mitty.

He changed forever.

Who doesn't daydream? Almost everyone does. Daydreaming is what happens when our mind wanders. According to neuroscientists, daydreaming is a brain state in which you are not actively engaged in any task, when your working memory is empty.[5] This happens more often than not; Harvard researchers Matthew Killingsworth and Daniel Gilbert found out we actually spend about 47 percent of our waking hours daydreaming on average, through their extensive research with about two thousand participants in 2010.[6]

In the study, Killingsworth and Gilbert first asked participants through notifications sent to their phones if they were engaged in whatever activities they were doing. Then they asked the second question to the participants if they were feeling pleasant, unpleasant, or neutral at that moment. Those 47 percent who responded they were not engaged in their current activities—daydreaming—answered they were significantly more unpleasant than when they focused on the activities. Based on this result, Killingsworth and Gilbert named their study "A Wandering Mind Is an Unhappy Mind."[7]

But daydreaming isn't all bad. Often, it augments creativity through divergent thinking, enabling us to come up with new ideas, as we saw in the previous chapter. In one study, researchers examined the content of what participants were thinking during mind-wandering, and they found that the mood of participants was more positive than negative if participants were *engaged* in interesting, off-task musings.[8] This points out the nuance with daydreaming; we might feel unpleasant when our mind wanders aimlessly. However, we could have positive experiences when we entertain certain ideas, albeit different from what we are doing at the moment, which is like the divergent thinking in the open mode.

While James Thurber's Walter Mitty daydreamed only throughout his life and stayed miserable in reality, Ben Stiller's Walter Mitty did not stop with daydreaming only; he engaged in his daydreams by testing them out. Thurber's Walter Mitty felt trapped in the humdrum of his life because he had *just* daydreamed about different identities. That would explain the satirical and unhappy tone of the story. Stiller's Walter Mitty could have been stuck with his mundane job, but he tried out things he was daydreaming about—searching for the photographer using bits of clues on the road in spite of many accidents, meeting all kinds of interesting people he wouldn't have met, and daring to go to dangerous places such as the Himalayas or Iceland with erupting volcanoes.

For Stiller's Walter Mitty, daydreaming worked as a divergent thinking to ideate, and his active engagement with different adventures were his experiments. That made his daydreaming a positive experience.

In this third perspective of the Placeholder, I am not asking you to quit your job and take the boldest adventures right now, as Stiller's Mitty did. The call to action here is to experiment your ideas like a mad scientist, however small they might be. You can start by experimenting with the smallest ideas and move on with more novel and bolder ideas as you keep going on.

As you iterate these experiments, you will learn something new and bring those insights back into learning for your next experiments. This process will help you filter out an idea or two as a prototype that you really want to pursue as your new career. Unlike in the movie, this process of experiments doesn't happen overnight or over a few days. It may take a couple of months or years to create a prototype you feel so aligned with based on values that matter to you and you are excited about. Yet, it can happen. Julia Child could attest to it.

JULIA CHILD'S PLACEHOLDER: A DECADE-LONG JOURNEY OF TRIAL AND ERROR

Julia Child is the iconic figure who introduced French cooking to the American public in the 1960s with the book *Mastering the*

Art of French Cooking. Although Julia Child is best known for her passion and achievement with French cooking in the US, she was never interested or serious about cooking or food until she had to go through the Placeholder of her own.

Long before she became a famous writer and French cuisine chef, Julia Child was an aspiring novelist in college, a copywriter for the advertising department of a luxury furniture brand, and an intelligence officer during World War II. During the war, her work on top secret assignments for the OSS (Office of the Strategic Service—the precursor of the modern CIA) took her to various places such as Washington, DC, Sri Lanka, and China. The OSS was disbanded as the war ended, and her assignment was over as well. Julia Child started thinking about her post-war career in 1946.[9]

Like her husband, Paul, who served during the war and continued his career in the United States Foreign Services, Julia Child could have joined him as well. However, she wanted to look for different ways to fulfill her creative and intellectual interests, dabbling in various activities, including writing. She didn't have a specific career path in mind; Julia Child was entering the Placeholder.

In 1948, Julia Child moved to Paris with her husband Paul, who got an assignment in France. There, Julia spent a year acclimating to life as a married woman and continuing to explore various hobbies. Nothing spoke to her creative and intellectual interests, except the French food. With Paul, who always appreciated fine cuisine, Julia got naturally interested in French cuisine. French cooking was fascinating to her, not only because of the quality of the food itself but the entire culinary culture—the care in preparation, the techniques involved, the philosophy of cooking as an art form, and the art of dining experience.

This experience was a sharp contrast to the culinary culture she was accustomed to in the US. Although Julia Child grew up in a wealthy family in California, she didn't experience the culinary culture much. In the early twentieth century in the US, people didn't consider dining a rich cultural experience but simply a necessity for life. Because of this difference, she found the rich culinary culture in French cuisine so intellectually and creatively captivating. Julia wanted to learn more about it. Although she was never seriously interested in cooking and didn't have much experience with it before coming to Paris, it being completely new territory for her didn't stop her. Julia Child was willing to try out more experiments with French cooking in the Placeholder.

But here's a quick quiz for you: From the moment Julia Child got interested in French cooking, how long do you think it took for her to establish herself as a chef?[10]

Ten years.

Yes, it took ten years for Julia Child to become the Julia Child we all know now. She didn't become a successful chef and cooking show host overnight. It took her about ten years of diverse experiments from 1951 to 1961.

In 1950, after Julia Child got serious about French cuisine, she started taking cooking classes in Paris for the first time. Initially, she faced many challenges due to her poor French. Being a woman in a male-dominated culinary world didn't help either. Despite these obstacles, her determination only grew stronger to learn more about French cooking. This led her to enroll at Le Cordon Bleu in 1951, one of the most prestigious culinary schools in the world.[11]

Julia Child tried multiple things on top of the professional training at Le Cordon Bleu. She joined an exclusive cooking club for women organized to support female chefs in a male-dominated professional culinary world. In this club, she met Simone Beck and Louisette Bertholle, forming lifelong friendships and professional partnerships with them. In 1953, with Simone and Louisette, Julia cofounded an informal cooking school, "L'École des Trois Gourmandes" ("The School of the Food Lovers"), to teach French cooking to American women living in Paris.[12]

In 1954, Julia Child started working on a French cookbook for an American audience with the cofounders of the informal cooking school. During much of the mid-1950s, Julia dedicated her time to extensive research, testing recipes, and teaching cooking classes. Going through so much trial and error, she was able to refine techniques and accumulated knowledge that would later be essential for her cookbook and cooking shows.[13]

In 1956, Julia and her coauthors made the first attempt at publishing the cookbook, but the publisher rejected it. It didn't deter Julia and her coauthors; they worked on updating the cookbook to make it more suitable for American measurements, ingredients, and kitchen appliances. Then, finally in October 1961, *Mastering the Art of French Cooking* was published to the American public. The book was met with critical acclaim and commercial success. This success led her to host a live cooking show on public TV, which lasted for more than three decades, until 1998. Julia Child became the leading figure in American culinary arts.[14]

This transformation from OSS officer to a celebrated chef was only possible thanks to all the experiments she did over a decade. These experiments were instrumental to Julia in building her confidence in teaching and her knowledge of French cuisines. It happened because of a series of divergent trials for her, planting seeds to host a cooking show on live TV in the future. Of course, she couldn't have predicted her future as it happened, but these experiments prepared her for it.

Her journey underscores the importance of exploration, openness to new and unfamiliar ideas, and willingness to experiment with them.

What's noteworthy is she didn't set out her experimental phase with a goal to become a leading figure in French cuisine. She might have daydreamed sometimes about what she would become in the process, but what she focused on was completely immersing herself in all the experiments, trying out different types of engagements—taking classes, joining or forming communities, teaching, and writing. This work met her needs for creative and intellectual interest, which mattered to her deeply. And eventually, this process of experiments guided Julia Child to become a pioneer who popularized French cuisine in the US.

HEATHER'S PLACEHOLDER: FROM REACTIVE TO PROACTIVE

Heather had daydreamed of leaving her home country, Canada, to work and live abroad since her childhood. She chose her major in university based on this dream. International relations was promising, as it might lead her to work in foreign services abroad. Unfortunately, she had to pass on that major because one of the prerequisites was economics, which she didn't want to take. Instead, she chose a major to become a teacher, thinking she could teach at international schools abroad.

After college, she got a job at a school in the Middle East; finally, her dream of living and working abroad came true. However, as soon as she started her dream job, she had to face the fact that she didn't enjoy teaching much. After a couple of years, Heather started looking for a new career—this time in publishing. Publishing was a big shift from teaching, but she got a job in sales at one of the biggest publishers in the world for their Dubai office. Although sales wasn't ideal for her, the job paid well with a lot of perks, including flexible time.

After four years in publishing sales, unfortunately, she bumped into another dead end and had to leave the company. Out of desperation, she took a job at another publishing company right away, although she sensed it wasn't the right decision from the beginning. Sadly, her intuition was correct and the company didn't last. Now she really had to leave the world of publishing and the Middle East altogether because her work visa expired.

Mentally, emotionally, and physically exhausted, Heather decided to take a month-long break from everything and flew to Thailand, where she always dreamed of visiting. That supposedly short trip turned into a three-year stint as a digital nomad. It wasn't what she had in mind even with the slightest possibility, but those three years of working as a digital nomad in Thailand became formative for Heather to learn about herself and what mattered to her. She was entering the Placeholder.

Until she went to Thailand, Heather knew nothing about the digital nomad lifestyle. Digital nomads are people who travel freely while working remotely using technology and the internet.[15] Fascinated by this new lifestyle, she jumped right into it. The freedom and flexibility of the digital nomad lifestyle offered great benefits; she could work anywhere and anytime to a certain degree. Most digital nomads were freelancers, so she could also pick who to work with or what to work on as well.

However, the same factors that offered freedom and flexibility became stressors for Heather because it was incredibly unstable with too much uncertainty. Her visa didn't allow her to stay for more than ninety days, so she had to leave Thailand and come back every three months. She had to always look for new clients and gigs to maintain a steady income and often worried about the shrinking balance in her savings account. Heather learned a certain level of stability was critical for her.

In spite of this instability and uncertainty, one clear benefit made it worth living as a digital nomad: a wide range of different jobs to experiment with. One time, she got involved in organizing the first conference for digital nomads in Chiang Mai in Thailand. Although she was getting fed up living as a digital nomad, Heather thoroughly enjoyed planning events with creative ideas, bringing three hundred fifty other digital nomads together.

During this experimental digital nomad phase in Thailand, Heather gleaned three factors that mattered to her work. First, flexibility of working—in flexible hours and locations. Second, some stability of life—without worrying about the next paycheck or next project. Lastly, the creative aspect of the work.

Even before she told me about her time in Thailand, I was already pretty impressed by her experiences of living in various parts of the world such as the Middle East and Southeast Asia and changing to different jobs from teaching to sales and freelancing. To me, she seemed always adventurous and proactive with her life, but her response surprised me in the interview.

"No, I think I was always reactive in the past. In university, I gave up the international relations major because I was afraid of getting a bad grade in economics, which was required for the degree. The situation was the same when I got the sales job in publishing; I knew I didn't like sales but still got the job that seemed okay. I could do it and got paid well. In all these decisions, I didn't take actions to move toward the thing that could be more ideal based on what mattered to me. Subconsciously, I think I was just waiting and hoping it would work out for me magically somehow."

She started changing through her experiments in Thailand. For example, she signed up for a class to learn about Facebook ads analytics. The course was technical and analytical, both of which she didn't revel in. Justifying it could be beneficial for her to get more potential digital marketing projects with analytics, she powered through it even though it was agonizing for her. After the course, she worked on some projects using Facebook ads, but the result wasn't great. In some cases, she didn't get paid or got fired from a gig.

Reflecting on that experience, Heather said, "What the fuck was I thinking? The job was not creative but technical and heavily reliant on data. I hated it. I got halfway through it, and I couldn't quit because of that sunk cost fallacy. I didn't really consider my actual interests or strengths." She had a long period of time with a lot of mistakes like that, but it became a fertile ground for growth based on so much learning. In Thailand, Heather finally allowed herself to be proactive with experiments such as taking classes, workshops, putting her hands on projects she never did, and interacting with other digital nomads from all over the world. She learned not to force herself to work based on the circumstances but started discerning what really mattered to her from what was simply available to her.

One day, she got a part-time job in digital marketing through an acquaintance of a friend. At first, her work was simply creating basic digital marketing materials for $15 per hour for the startup. The client, founder of the startup, really liked working with her and eventually hired her to be the first head of marketing for the company. Now her experiment evolved to another level; developing and running an entire marketing department was a different game. This opportunity served her well for what mattered to her: flexibility (it was a fully remote job), stability (it was a full-time job), and the creative energy from bringing people together (it involved a lot of out of the box communication and event planning with others).

After going through a series of experiments, now she could narrow down a few critical ones. "So in a really long, dramatic, roundabout way, I got to the place where I feel like I probably should have started out. But also, if I had gone into marketing fifteen years ago, marketing looked very different then, so perhaps this was how it was supposed to be." Heather smiled.

She thinks she's still in the Placeholder, but with a different point of view about career from when she started. She said, "It's rare to expect your ultimate career is only one step away; in reality, it always takes multiple steps to get there. You might want to be an entrepreneur, but you can't just spring to that. You might have to do many different kinds of work as bridging steps toward the career you want. I feel more comfortable taking my current job even though it's not my 'dream job' because now I understand the concept of shaping something I want, step by step. I didn't quite understand how it worked in the past. The moment I realized it wasn't what I wanted, I used to just quit or leave. Now I feel like I have far more patience and a long-term view."

Heather's is a quintessential Placeholder story. Like an anthropologist, she observed her experiences and decoded what mattered to her through many experiments in the Middle East and Thailand. Like a designer, she ideated in her own creative way; she designed her own path. She took classes and workshops, upskilled herself, and tested out working as a digital nomad in Thailand. Like a mad scientist, she experimented on repeat—from event planning to digital marketing part-time and leading a marketing team.

Through the Placeholder, Heather finally found her own way to guide herself more proactively rather than daydreaming, waiting, and hoping. "Now it's different. Every work I take on is like a 'project' that I *choose* to do based on what matters to me rather than being forced by the circumstances," she said with clarity. Heather continues to experiment to fine-tune her "prototype" in her Placeholder.

✪ GUIDE: HOW TO EXPERIMENT LIKE A MAD SCIENTIST

When it comes to being like a mad scientist, one of the biggest traps many people fall into is infinite ideation without taking real actions. Focusing on ideating only can create inertia because you are afraid of the potential costs from trying them out, such as failure, time consumption, and other opportunity costs that may incur. But nothing happens with ideas alone. Don't let your good daydreams die as James Thurber's Walter Mitty did. Give life to it instead, as did Ben Stiller's Walter Mitty. Here is some inspiration on how to experiment with your ideas like a mad scientist.

1. SPREAD THE WORD!
- Spread the word to others about your ideas you want to experiment with. You might have a group of close friends or coworkers who are supportive of you no matter what. Tell them about the new ideas you want to try out and openly ask for support or invite them to be a part of your experiment. Create your own cheerleaders; don't do it alone.
- You can also try it with strangers, if you think they resonate with what you are trying to do. Sometimes strangers are more effective in giving you unbiased feedback on how to experiment than people who know you well. Connecting with strangers for the experiment you'd like to run is also a good way to learn more about other ways to test your ideas.
- Spreading the word is important because it helps you build momentum, setting you in motion to experiment. Also, it creates accountability for you to follow through with results. Don't be self-conscious. Remember, you are wearing the hat of a mad scientist who doesn't care about what others think or say.

2. START WITH THE EASIEST OPTION
- If you have no qualms about experimenting with the most daring and adventurous idea, by all means, go for it. But also know that you don't have to start with the boldest one. If one of your ideas is to start a YouTube channel for books that made a huge impact on you, you don't have to hire a professional YouTube video production company and upload every week right away. You can start experimenting by posting a series of book reviews on social media or blogs. It'll be easier than starting a full YouTube channel from the get-go, and you can keep building on easy ideas.
- The point is to *not* overwhelm yourself by trying to experiment with the most "perfect" way right away. That approach is the fastest way to failure. The key here is to build momentum with experiments, not to perfect them.

3. DOCUMENT: ACTION AND LEARNING
- As you are doing all kinds of experiments, start documenting what you are doing and what you are learning from each experiment. This step is optional, but I found this personally important because it creates a natural internal feedback loop between what matters to you and further ideation. Therefore, it will make your experiments better as you document your frustrations and takeaways from the experience.
- This experiment stage often feels quite chaotic; you are doing these experiments on top of your life, which is still going on at full speed. If you do not give yourself time to pause and reflect on what you are doing and learning, it's easy to get lost and unmotivated with your experiences. You can document every week, every month, or even every three months. And you can choose different methods of documentation—writing, voice recording, or video recording. Choose an easy method for you and document regularly.

You might wonder how your experiments would lead up to something as grand as what Julia Child achieved or what Heather came to do, living in many countries and trying out different professions. You might even think your small experiments look "feeble" compared to theirs. I hear you, but I want to challenge that notion as the "hindsight bias."

Hindsight bias was first studied by Baruch Fischhoff, an American academic specialized in decision theory at Carnegie Mellon University.[16] Also known as "creeping determinism," it occurs when people feel that they "knew it all along," as they perceive past events as having been more predictable than they were.[17]

Looking back at what Julia Child did during those ten years of experiments, if you say, "Of course, it was obvious she would become successful," you are seeing it with a hindsight bias. When she began learning about French cuisine in 1951, she didn't aim to make French cuisine accessible to the American public. She didn't envision a magnificent finish line as a goal for many feeble and grand experiments she did over a decade. Her experiments let her bring French cuisine to the American audience eventually, but no one could have predicted it, including herself.

The same was true for Heather; she couldn't have predicted she would be interested in leading digital marketing. She discovered creativity as one of the factors that mattered to her through experiments and is continuing to refine her prototype. No one who has been through the Placeholder "knew it all along" or was destined to succeed.

When Ben Stiller's *The Secret Life of Walter Mitty* was released to the critics and public, it got mixed reviews. One of the reasons was because it didn't have any grand "third act" or conclusion at the end, even after Walter Mitty took all the adventurous actions. The conclusion was anticlimactic, not following the typical Hollywood formula. But I cannot think of a better ending because it highlighted the adventurous journey of Walter Mitty, not the final outcome of what he became.

If I were to imagine an "epilogue" for Ben Stiller's Walter Mitty, I bet he continues to experiment with his life with an open and free mind, without feeling any regrets or anxieties about the "unlived life" or "goals he could have achieved." In the Placeholder, your mindset shifts from a goal-driven, deductive way of life to a more expansive approach—one that embraces everything as an experiment, free from expectation.

*****

You come to acquire many great qualities as a result of the Placeholder. At the same time, some features of the Placeholder make you think it's a dangerous place to be, like a shady back alley. Not only Ben Stiller's Walter Mitty but also everyone who has been through the Placeholder would have loved to know about what to be aware of before they stepped in it. So would I. In the next chapter, we'll look into some obstacles in the Placeholder you should be aware of and how to manage them.

CHAPTER 7

The Illusive Obstacles of the Placeholder

So far, we explored so much from what makes you enter the Placeholder, what's at stake for us, and how to go through it skillfully by taking three different perspectives as an anthropologist, a designer, and a mad scientist. Through my story and those of Katie, Greg, Amit, Ben Stiller's Walter Mitty, Julia Child, and Heather, you could see there were no right or wrong ways to reflect, ideate, and experiment in the Placeholder. They didn't follow a single "playbook."

The fact that there is nothing to hold on to or reference can create a lot of mental and emotional barriers. Had I known a little more about these obstacles of the Placeholder, I would not have let them hold me back with self-doubt, anxiety, and worries. Although what happens during the Placeholder is different for people, here are some common illusive obstacles you may encounter and how to manage them.

1. EXTREMELY UNSETTLING: DON'T BE TRAPPED IN THE SUNK COST FALLACY

The Placeholder can be chaotic and unsettling. Although I knew I needed to change something about my tech executive career, it took me such a long time to justify the change because I had invested so much time, money, and effort to build it up over fifteen years. *Is it reasonable for me to try to do something else when my current career cost me so much in the past? Why would I revoke my past efforts?* These thoughts held me back.

In fact, I didn't have to make my past efforts invalid; I needed to be mindful of the "sunk cost fallacy." In economics, a sunk cost—also known as retrospective cost—is a cost that has already been incurred and cannot be recovered.[1] In other words, a sunk cost is the sum paid in the past that is no longer relevant to decisions about the future. My expensive MBA degree and tech career in which I invested so much time and effort had served me well up to that point, but those past sunk costs would not be relevant to my future career.

This sunk cost fallacy often holds us back from making rational decisions in our everyday life. We can remain in failing relationships because we have already invested too much in them to leave. Some think a war must continue because the lives of those who died in the war would have been sacrificed in vain unless victory is achieved. This is clearly not a rational way to make decisions for the future. However, we often stay with the status quo because going into the *unknown* future with a clearly *known* sunk cost from the past feels extremely unsettling. The resistance from the sunk cost fallacy makes it harder to enter the Placeholder in the beginning.

It's worth being aware of this when you notice reluctance to change, in spite of the fact that you have a desperate urge to change. It's a trap.

2. URGENT AND INEVITABLE: DO NOT CONFUSE SIGNAL WITH NOISE

Although the sunk cost fallacy might hold you back, the Placeholder would still look "urgent and inevitable" to you. This sense of urgency occurs because you know what you have been doing doesn't serve you anymore and you need a different way to help yourself. You find it necessary to go through this phase of exploration, although it's so uncertain and scary.

However, misinterpreting what is urgently called for is also easy. Because of urgency, you might focus on *finding* the right work for you as soon as possible with little exploration and experiments. Such noises can easily fill up the Placeholder, but the real signal you need to pay attention to is your deep longing for what makes you fully alive.

This decision is hard for any profession but especially for teachers, doctors, or lawyers, careers in which you are highly specialized in a single career track and expected to stay on it with few changes. Regardless, when you stop feeling the engagement and energy from your career, it's an inevitable signal to drop the myth of specialization and enter the Placeholder.

3. UNCERTAIN AND CHAOTIC: ACCEPT IT'S NATURALLY NONLINEAR AND IDIOSYNCRATIC

You will encounter many moments of uncertainty throughout the entire Placeholder as you manage various new ideas and experiments. Particularly in the beginning, you might find it directionless or out of focus with seemingly random ideas and tests; therefore, it could also feel chaotic. This feeling is natural because the Placeholder is a nonlinear and idiosyncratic process.

While you are experimenting with new ideas, you can't see or feel the progress in a straightforward way. You often prove your hypothesis about a certain work idea to be wrong as you test them, which may send you many steps backward. It's nonlinear. You will also test many new ideas that seem inconsistent with other ideas. Or you might get negative feedback from people around you because what you are trying to do is so unfamiliar from what you used to do.

Since the Placeholder is idiosyncratic for each person, it may stay uncertain and chaotic without revealing any clear pattern or path for a while. I was all over the place, trying out so many random things at the same time. Especially in the beginning, when I didn't know what to do or where to start, the first set of ideas that came to my mind was about how to suffer less from work for myself. Thinking of finding meaningful work was a stretch goal at that point. Below is the list of things I tried randomly to alleviate my suffering without any expectations:

- Applied for different jobs inside Meta and at other companies, with the faint hope it could solve my problem. This solution was always my first go-to—and a familiar—one whenever I felt stuck with my work. Finding: Although I got to work on seemingly interesting projects, the sense of "meh" was still present. I learned the lesson that I really shouldn't resort to this solution anymore.
- Took classes on emotional intelligence and compassion, hoping it would balance me better. Finding: It helped me understand why I suffered at work better, as I got to have higher clarity of my mental and emotional reactions to various situations. Still, I wasn't sure how to apply the insight to create meaningful work. It hinted that perhaps I should find a way to incorporate learnings from these courses into my work.
- Went on many yoga and silent meditation retreats to practice mindfulness for days and weeks. Finding: I felt better during and right after the retreats, although it didn't last when I came back to work. It brought up a question: "What can make the sense of well-being last?"
- Had vulnerable conversations with the HR and my leadership teams about my predicament; I was *miserable* at my *good* job in this *great* company. Finding: They suggested some solutions, such as going on a longer vacation or taking leadership coaching or changing teams. I knew those solutions might treat symptoms but not the actual problem. They couldn't really help, and I grew more frustrated.
- Had countless coffee chats with people in different teams at work and in other industries—from health care to entertainment—to

collect some ideas about how they help people stop suffering at work. Finding: They all agreed with the need to help people to have a sense of well-being at work, but most ideas were around what people could do individually for themselves. I started wondering what could be a more systemic solution.

- Got certified as a yoga teacher, emotional intelligence trainer for the Search Inside Yourself course, compassion facilitator for the Compassion Cultivation Training at Stanford, and many other courses. Finding: The investment in terms of time, money, and energy to take all these courses while working full-time was big, but I learned so much. I still wasn't sure what to do with them eventually, but I started dreaming of teaching them at work.

These are just a few examples of everything I did for two and a half years, but the ideas and experiments evolved over time in a nonlinear way. I started dabbling in something that could help me feel better at work and got more serious with other ideas. In this earlier part of the Placeholder process, I met so many other people suffering at work as I was. However, most companies, regardless of industries, haven't truly solved this problem and they took it for granted as if the sense of languishing and low engagement were just the way things were at work. They were offering great employee perks—for example, massage machine at work, many training programs, team off-sites, and coaching services, etc.—to alleviate symptoms, but they weren't truly treating the problem.

On the surface, I felt as if I was getting even more lost with so many things I tried in this nonlinear process. However, all the takeaways and insights from these ideas and experiments were pushing me to a certain direction—to do something about solving the employee suffering at work systematically. As I didn't have a degree in organizational culture or experience in human resource, this seemed like overstretching myself, but I found it deeply meaningful.

4. JUDGING AND INTIMIDATING: DON'T EVALUATE WHEN YOU INNOVATE

Going through the Placeholder can be like going through a dark tunnel without knowing how long the tunnel is. In such a dark tunnel, your sneaky "saboteurs" can become active in your mind. These undetected inner critics may judge you and your Placeholder experiments heavily and threaten that you are making a mistake. Because of these qualities, the Placeholder doesn't have a good reputation culturally and socially.

Often, the Placeholder creates a career break in your résumé or makes your career look "inconsistent" by jumping from a teacher to a content manager for a startup. Socially indoctrinated that you must always continue to build a career in a *logical* way, the inner judge would criticize having any gap or inconsistency. Listening to this saboteur, you might think, "How do I explain this to my future employer or to anyone?" as it feels like you are "off the track."

Another popular story told by saboteurs during the Placeholder is that you are wasting time on something you don't know how to derive value from for your future career. When you are working full-time as a software engineer but the most meaningful work in your mind is pottery making, this voice of saboteur criticizes your half-heartedness in your full-time career. It intimidates you for violating the social code of driving toward goals and maximizing efficiency because you don't know *yet* how pottery making would be valuable for your future career.

In the Placeholder where you are constantly innovating with your insights, ideas, and experiments, you can be often vulnerable to these inner critics. To protect your actions in the Placeholder from any sabotages such as criticism and intimidation, remember to pause any conclusive evaluation of your ideas or experiments. Saboteurs make it tempting to assess how your Placeholder experience will contribute to your future, but you cannot evaluate the outcome when you innovate. The inner critics will use the past judgment to limit your ideas and experiments. Instead, keep coming up with as many ideas as possible, whether they're big, small, completely wacky, or mundane. Don't let your saboteurs enter through the back door of evaluation during the innovation.[2]

*****

As you go along in the Placeholder, if you find it extremely unnerving, that's completely understandable. Seeing everything from the sunk cost fallacy in the beginning of the Placeholder is easy, but move forward with ideas and experiments. The Placeholder is also uncertain and chaotic by nature because it is nonlinear and idiosyncratic for everyone. However unsettling it is, you won't be able to ignore the nudges from the Placeholder that demand you to take innovative actions. And you will have saboteurs that make you doubt your ideas and actions. You'll have to practice talking back to your saboteurs, saying, "Thank you, but no thank you for now," and keep ideating.

As you become fully aware of these qualities of the Placeholder, you will be able to skillfully navigate it with calm and resilience. These qualities are illusive obstacles that become powerful once you are mindful of them.

STEPH'S PLACEHOLDER: WHAT IS POSSIBLE?

Steph Stern is an excellent coach specialized in applying Internal Family Systems into her practice. But this wasn't what she had in mind when she started her career in green energy after graduate school, as I learned in the interview.

Steph was dedicated to educating people and organizations to advocate for green energy initiatives and helping local governments shape policies around them. She went to get a master's degree at MIT in City Planning and Environmental Policy so she could better contribute to this work. She started working at her "dream job" at a local government agency supporting cities with energy efficiency policies and programs. Unfortunately, frustration crept in soon after Steph started the job, disappointing her. *I couldn't believe this is what it was going to be,* she thought.

The agency was not doing well, as it was going through a transitional period. Longtime staff at the organization were unhappy with the leadership and were visibly disengaged. The projects Steph was hired to work on were stalled. Demoralized and unsettled, she started doubting her career decision: "What if this path of green energy work isn't for me?" She thought she might have to rethink everything after investing her time, money, and efforts in graduate school.

The first thing that came to her mind was quitting and finding a new job right away, but it didn't feel right to leave the job she just got. She wanted to be thoughtful about financial stability and her future career. Although it wasn't ideal, she decided to stick around and explore other options in the meantime. Steph was entering her "Placeholder," in retrospect, experimenting with new ideas and activities to create the right input for her.

Steph formed a women's career group with a friend to share struggles at work with one another. She also co-launched a blog to write about career, identity, personal growth, etc. for many years. Volunteering for a crisis hotline, résumé reviews, and interview preps for people who wanted to get a job in the green energy industry was another form of experiment. When she set out to engage in all these activities, she didn't exactly plan them or have any expectations about how they might turn out. A lot of activities were random at first and happened in unstructured ways. Doing these experiments, though, she learned all these activities had a common thread—they were about people and dealing with feelings/emotions.

Steph could find a trace of this thread back to her graduate school. "During graduate school, I took a short course on mediation training. That wasn't even a major part of my graduate program, but it immediately hooked me because of what I could do by understanding how people felt and working with them through their emotions," she reflected.

The career group and blog turned out to be great channels to help others process emotions as they went through turbulent times at work. In her volunteering, she found it so meaningful to help people going through difficult phases in their lives—for example, crisis or recruiting for a new job in uncertainty—and their emotional journey with it. Around the same time, she registered in a coach training in order to learn more about herself and how to help others better in their emotionally tumultuous life and work.

In the beginning of these many random, idiosyncratic, and uncertain experiments, Steph wasn't sure what a career of working with people and their emotions would look like. Nonetheless, she continued to follow what she found interesting and meaningful. Learning from various experiences in this Placeholder, she got to affirm her intuition slowly and gradually. Eventually, this process of trial and error based on her intrinsic motivation led her to shape up a path for a new career.

She took the first formal step into this by joining the Search Inside Yourself Leadership Institute, "SIYLI" in short. The institute facilitated programs to develop emotional intelligence based on neuroscience and mindfulness practices for leaders in various organizations. Originally, Steph intended to stay on this job only for a year, as another experiment. After all, she ended up staying at the SIYLI for over six years, learning, expanding her expertise on emotional intelligence, managing people, and growing into the leadership.

Steph could witness firsthand at SIYLI how critical it was for leaders to develop emotional intelligence for everything they did. In her own leadership position, she also enjoyed playing the role of a coach for her team. Through the coach training, Steph deeply appreciated the power of helping people be aware of dynamics of many inner parts. Now she could interweave all these threads of insights to craft a new career for herself, helping people navigate challenges in life and work by understanding the emotional kaleidoscope of their inner selves. As this new career path was further crystallized, she left SIYLI to dedicate her time to coaching using Internal Family Systems.

Steph's story shows what's possible when you are willing to explore what is meaningful for you, without imposing on yourself to make a career out of it. Now, she is deeply engaged in her work and ready to evolve her career as a coach based on intrinsic motivation. This makes her an excellent coach, in return.

Steph created this virtuous circle through the Placeholder. She was willing to question her old assumptions and delved deeper into understanding her own new "why" through trial and errors of various experiments. She followed what was meaningful to her, and each experiment became a thread for her to craft a new garment of career that fits her better.

*****

What the Placeholder promises is not a perfect job without any problems. You will always have some challenges to manage in your career, even with the Placeholder. But the Placeholder shows you how to get unstuck with your work that doesn't serve you anymore. With this virtuous circle of insights, ideas, and experiments, you don't need to struggle anymore but reinvent yourself.

That's possible in the Placeholder.

PART 3

CHAPTER 8

From the Placeholder to Noble Work

The good life is a process, not a state of being. It is a direction, not a destination.
—CARL ROGERS

My tantrum on the shuttle in 2016 implanted an idea that I needed to take care of myself to stop suffering from work in a different way from the past. That led me to play with all kinds of self-development ideas and try out some of them too. In that process, I noticed how many people were in the same situation as me, afflicted by languishing and meaninglessness in their career. At the organizational level, this translated into symptoms such as the lack of engagement and satisfaction of employees, directly affecting the productivity and efficiency of businesses. These themes were recurring for many teams at Meta, and there were many initiatives brought up by the HR team to solve the problem, but the problem persisted.

My experiment expanded to do something about the well-being of the organization beyond myself. I hypothesized that the systematic effort to increase the self-awareness of individuals and psychological safety within teams might address the problem. If people are trained to be well aware of their thoughts and feelings, they could manage themselves better and relate with one another more skillfully. As a result, people could have difficult conversations without damaging the relationships and be more compassionate with one another in conflicts. This would naturally contribute to building the foundation for psychological safety within teams.

Sharing this idea around the company, I got plugged in to facilitate more workshops and training sessions for teams. I created programs based on everything I was trained and started testing them with more individuals and teams. It felt as if I was bootstrapping my own startup within the company. The more I engaged in my "startup" experiments, the more motivated I got. I could see the impact of programs; people finally understood their ultimate potential and saw their coworkers as whole people for the first time.

In this process, I came to envision a workplace where we could all achieve something wonderful without harming ourselves with harshness in the name of productivity and results only. My daydream got bolder. *Maybe I can contribute to creating such a workplace culture!* When this vision became so clear in 2022, I left Meta and founded my own business, People+Culture. It was my "Noble Work."

As you go through the Placeholder, you come to crystallize the kind of work you find meaningful. That's Noble Work. It's not noble because it's superior to other works. The word "noble" means "to come to know" in its Latin root "gnobilis."[1] Noble Work is not the job or role you choose among what's available but what you create through many experiments in the Placeholder. You do *not find* your Noble Work but *craft, define, shape, develop, or create* it. You come to know it that way.

JENN'S PLACEHOLDER: CRAFTING, DEFINING, SHAPING, DEVELOPING, AND CREATING HER OWN NOBLE WORK

The notion we could craft, define, develop, shape, or even create our Noble Work came more naturally to Jenn Yee earlier than it did for me. Jenn is a learning and organizational development consultant. Like many others you have seen in this book, she also created her own Noble Work through many experiments in the Placeholder phase.

"I was always skeptical when anyone said, 'Find your own passion,'" Jenn said in the interview. It didn't resonate with her early on in her life. She had the same experience during the business school when her peers were saying they were passionate about XYZ positions in ABC companies so earnestly in interviews for summer internships. The widespread pressure to find work that somehow unfolded from "passions" really bothered her. When you're early in your career, how would you even know what you're truly passionate about? And should that drive your career choices?

Jenn was more interested in finding meaning, rather than passion, in work. She said, "I could always change my career in different directions to align with what was meaningful to me at the time." For Jenn, work was a vehicle to do meaningful things that aligned with her personal values. Her approach was certainly different from the common operating belief in the business world: "Find your passion and keep working on it and then you can have a successful career."

Identifying what was meaningful to work on wasn't easy, so she started with a job in consulting for practical reasons, like many of her classmates did after business school. Yet she began experimenting right away for random ideas she found valuable from her own experience. Having struggled through the ancillary parts of business school herself—networking, personal finance, dating—she had an idea to create a virtual space for MBA students and graduates to share their tips for how to navigate life during and after business school.

This idea led to an experiment, MBAsocial.com. She created an online media company that provided business school students with national content about relationships, family, health, style, career, and school life in a fun, relatable, and accessible way. She found it meaningful to create a support infrastructure for business school students even after they graduated. The site served as the definitive survival guide for getting through business school life, with over thirty contributing writers from the top fifteen MBA programs in the US.

Working on her first startup while moonlighting in a consulting job was challenging but also energizing. She could see the impact from her work directly with those projects. Whether it was the readers, customers, or people working together with her, she found it meaningful that she could help others directly. She immediately felt drawn to working in a startup.

The strong rapport she built with other startup founders in the Chicago area, combined with her penchant for giving advice and support to peers who were unsure of navigating the post-MBA world, led her to another experiment. She took a role as a founding director at the Startup Institute in Chicago. Startup Institute helped individuals develop the skills, mindset, and network to get jobs and thrive in startup and high-growth companies. Launching the Chicago chapter for Startup Institute, Jenn deeply resonated with helping others find their way to fulfilling work in the local startup and high-growth tech firms through strong partnerships she formed with them.

Noble Work became clearer for Jenn through these experiments. Before, the work was what enabled her to have a direct impact on others. Now, Noble Work meant helping people find the work they were interested in and found meaningful. This led her to another experiment: She applied for a role in organizational development at a startup. But one clear problem was Jenn did not have any previous experience in organizational development or HR. In general, you were expected to have experience in the field of corporate HR to apply for such a role. This would have been enough reason to stop most people from applying for the job, but it didn't stop her. She reflected on this new experiment in our discussion.

"Sure, I didn't have specific organizational development experience on my résumé, but in some ways that made it feel less risky to go for it. I could see the connection between my prior experience and the job description clearly: Helping people develop themselves to do what they find meaningful was important to me and I believed I could do the work inside an organization based on my previous experiments at Startup Institute and with my own media company. What's the worst that could happen? If I get rejected, I will try something else!"

And she was right. Not only did she get the job, but she successfully developed and led the entire learning and development, employee engagement and experience, and organizational development team at the startup—later acquired by HelloFresh—for the following four years. After leaving the startup, Jenn Yee is currently offering consulting to companies and leaders on topics of organizational culture and strategy, career development, learning, internal communications, and employee engagement. She's continuing with her Noble Work—helping people perform better, feel happier, and get engaged at work.

THE VIRTUOUS CYCLE OF THE PLACEHOLDER, NOBLE WORK, AND SELF-EFFICACY

Jenn's Placeholder experiences toward her Noble Work is a great example of self-efficacy. In 1997, the psychologist Albert Bandura introduced self-efficacy in human development. He defined it as "the belief in one's capabilities to organize and execute the sources of action required to manage prospective situations."[2]

Self-efficacy is a more critical driver than self-esteem for us to create a Noble Work. While self-esteem is an overall emotional evaluation of one's worth and value, self-efficacy is about feeling competent in our actions in specific areas. Although both self-esteem and self-efficacy seem helpful in making us more confident in our own abilities, self-efficacy is more effective in building confidence concretely.

According to Bandura, self-efficacy plays a major role in how you approach goals, tasks, and challenges. To develop this, two important factors come into play: observational learning and social experiences.[3] These two factors explain how you get to strengthen self-efficacy further in the context of the Placeholder to shape your Noble Work, as you learn by observing yourself and doing experiments in the social context.

For Jenn, her self-efficacy became the baseline capacity to kick-start her Placeholder, as shown when she started her first startup while working on her consulting job. She didn't believe in "finding your own passion" first; instead, she started an experiment with what she found meaningful at the time, and it didn't have to be her main job.

Furthermore, Jenn strengthened her self-efficacy as she dove deeper into her Placeholder with more new attempts to become a founding director of the Startup Institute and work as a learning and development leader at another startup without prior HR experience. Through each of these new experiments, she was able to clarify her Noble Work: helping people perform better, feel happier, and get engaged at work.

With high self-efficacy, you are more likely to view difficult tasks as something to be experienced and mastered rather than to be avoided because they are new, Bandura says.[4] Jenn's case clearly shows that her initial self-efficacy was a great enabler for her Placeholder because she didn't avoid trying anything new. But please don't worry if you don't think you have a strong baseline self-efficacy like Jenn. That's what the Placeholder is for; you get to practice and develop it through intentional experiments.

As your experiments go on in the Placeholder, your self-efficacy will strengthen. Consequently, you will be able to reinvent yourself aligned with your Noble Work. You want to be like this; self-efficacy builds the ultimate confidence in your adaptability for any kinds of experiments. The Placeholder, Noble Work, and self-efficacy create a virtuous cycle for you to keep growing with your meaningful works.

JOSHUA'S PLACEHOLDER: NOBLE WORK TO BE FULLY HUMAN

As they say, "like attracts like," the Placeholder attracts another Placeholder. That's how Joshua Steinfeldt and I met for the first time, in our respective Placeholders. Joshua wears many hats as a professional coach, mindfulness teacher, host of *The Courageous Life* podcast, and cofounder of Adagio, a purpose-driven community of coaches. In all his works, he makes you feel seen, heard, and safe with his warm voice, genuine curiosity, and calming presence.

As an experienced coach, he is deeply interested in helping people unlock their potential. As a host of the podcast, he invites world-renowned thought leaders and teachers into deep and authentic conversations about what matters most. As a mindfulness teacher, he helps people deepen awareness and get curious about their inner landscapes. Everything he does is to help people craft ways of living and working that bring them a sense of being fully alive while they are here. This work is his Noble Work. How did he come to create this?

Joshua always wanted to help people, but he wasn't sure how or what to do about it. One day after graduating from college, he got a call from a friend about an open health coaching role. He didn't know what that was exactly, but he applied and got the job. Joshua moved to San Diego for it and met a master coach named Julie Somerville who had helped develop the coaching program he would be a part of. In the first encounter with Julie, Joshua had one of those "crystallizing moments"[5] when it just clicked with him and made him think, *This is it!*

When Joshua walked in the door and met Julie, she asked him, "How are you?"

Joshua responded as usual, "I am fine."

And Julie asked again, "No, how are you really doing?"

She was genuinely curious about how Joshua was, and her curiosity drew him into the conversation immediately. Working with her, Joshua learned the art and mindset of coaching: asking questions, being genuinely curious, and listening deeply. The way of coaching—walking beside people instead of trying to fix or solve them—was so revelatory to him. He fell in love with the mastery of coaching.

From that moment onward, Joshua coached, taught, and facilitated workshops for over a decade. He didn't know exactly what shape his meaningful work would take, but he intuited it would be a form of service. Joshua realized a perfect role didn't exist. His role models such as Rick Hanson and Mark Nepo had shown the wilderness was crossable, but it was up to him to blaze his own trail. He had to keep trying things out and pay careful attention to insights he learned on the path until it became clearer.

In every experiment along the way, he looked for a sense of alignment by being attentive to how each experience felt emotionally and physically. He explained this process in the interview:

> Feeling out of alignment was a signal to let go of things that didn't serve me anymore. When I felt burned out, I had an intense period of asking myself questions like "What am I getting from this?" and "What would make me feel really alive?" I listened deeply to myself for answers. After listening for a while, I knew I had to go try something else. It was time to bet on myself. I didn't know exactly what it was going to look like though, so I began experimenting.

One perspective that boosted his experiments came from one of his mentors, Rick Hanson, the renowned psychologist and meditation teacher. He offered Joshua a suggestion: What if he designed every aspect of work he was involved in as an "accelerant" for the meaningful work he'd like to do ultimately? Joshua took this advice to heart. "All the work I have intentionally chosen to do—my podcast, teaching, and coaching—are accelerants that help me build toward what I want to do in the world. It's a journey, and I know it will take many different shapes. But this is the work; I don't want to do anything else," Joshua reflected with gentle clarity in his eyes.

Now, Joshua thinks of everything he does as accelerants, as he is diligently continuing to develop and refine his Noble Work. He exudes the ultimate growth mindset in his path of mastery as a coach, podcast host, mindfulness teacher, and community builder. He is always open to learning and evolving with his Noble Work. This reflects what he wants to *become* as a whole person. No separation exists between what he does and who he is. His Noble Work feeds who he is becoming, and that also shapes his Noble Work in return. A deep congruence between his inner and outer life is present.

NOBLE WORK CAN BE TRULY NOBLE

In the process of interviewing many people in the Placeholder, an interesting theme emerged: Most Noble Works of my interviewees were about serving others or at least had an element of service.

Joshua's Noble Work is helping others unlock their potential and motivating them with courage to stay resilient on their path. His coaching practice, podcast, and meditation training are all different expressions of his Noble Work. For Jenn, her Noble Work is helping people perform better, feel happier, and get engaged at work. For Amit, who we met in Chapter 5, he wants to create an indoor pickleball court to let his community come together even in the cold winter.

It didn't apply to all interviewees, but out of the fifteen people I interviewed, thirteen cases fell into the realm of service when it came to their Noble Works. It was as if Noble Work helped them actualize and furthermore guided them to transcend their own needs and be willing to contribute to the world. Could this be true?

Dr. Abraham Maslow seemed to have noticed something similar to this and thought about it sixty years ago. You might know him through the "Maslow's Hierarchy of Needs,"[6] which is about five distinct human needs stacked up in a pyramid, with safety at the bottom, belonging/love and self-esteem in between, and self-actualization at the top. When he introduced this concept in his 1943 paper, he described self-actualization as the peak experience of human needs when we achieve our truest potential, feeling fulfilled as a result.[7]

Maslow's Hierarchy - Earlier Version

Image by Miroo Kim

However, in his later years, Maslow observed that "transcendence" was another need on top of self-actualization. Transcendence was the moment when people realized they were motivated by higher values. He discovered that many self-actualizing individuals experienced moments of transcendence frequently. He noted that these individuals had a deep sense of who they were and how they wanted to contribute to the world.[8]

Maslow found it paradoxical at first that so many self-actualizing individuals were so selfless, with such a strong desire to actualize their own potential. In 1961, Maslow concluded that self-actualization might be a transitional goal, a step along the path to the transcendence of identity. What happened in this transition from self-actualization to transcendence wasn't about "self" anymore. To capture this, Maslow preferred using the term being "fully human" instead of self-actualization.[9]

```
         ▲
       ╱Trans╲
      ╱cend   ╲
     ╱ Self-   ╲
    ╱Actualization╲
   ╱───────────────╲
  ╱  Self-Esteem    ╲
 ╱───────────────────╲
╱  Belonging & Love   ╲
```

Maslow's Hierarchy - Updated Version

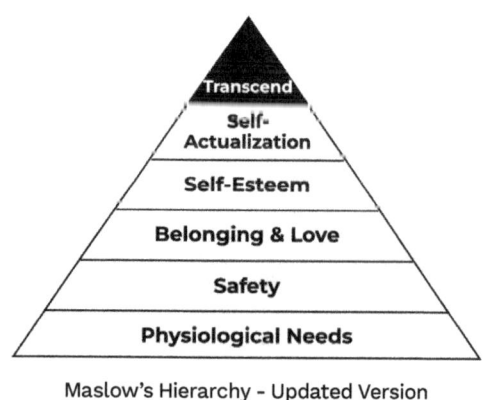

Image by Miroo Kim

Being *fully human* entails that you actualize full potential by understanding and accepting yourself wholly—for the good, the bad, and everything in between. Being fully human, you are motivated to do your best to unlock your potential for yourself and others as well. This was the common quality of Noble Work people shared in the Placeholder; it wasn't only for themselves but for others too. Jenn and Joshua both chose to do many experiments, as they were highly driven to be fully human themselves. Yet what they wanted through their Noble Works was to serve others as well so they could also be fully human.

THE TRUE MEANING OF NOBLE WORK

Noble Work is not a vocation you are *called* to do, nor is it a single career you must keep doing for the rest of your life. Although viewing it as a goal or a final destination is easy because you construct your Noble Work through the Placeholder, it's neither. You don't do it only because it excites you like passion or it gives you an absolute meaning for your life, like purpose. Noble Work is not forced upon you either.

Through the stories of mine and many people in this book, you can tell that Noble Work may not be only a specific job, work, or career but more like your intention. You might be working in a series of different professions but under a coherent theme of what matters to you. It may manifest in various forms and scopes—your professional career, a side job, a passion project, a hobby, or even in the way you relate with others. However it shows up, it carries an intrinsic value for you.

At first, this intention might be completely unknown to you. As you dedicate time and effort to things you find meaningful, each time this intention gets emboldened, it eventually manifests itself clearly to you as your Noble Work. Your experiments in the Placeholder are catalysts to manifest it.

Entering the Placeholder, you are following your innate needs to achieve self-actualization, to become your truest potential with your work. This path helps you establish the genuine peace between who you are becoming and what you do in the world. As you deeply engage in the Placeholder and create your Noble Work, you'll feel alive and content each moment, living honestly to your "why," no matter what's happening around you. This deep sense of congruence with your *why*, I dare to say, is the ultimate source of well-being with your career.

I remember feeling a chasm between my inner and outer life as I entered the Placeholder. Although my outer life looked pretty good, on track for success with a good job in a prestigious company, I was utterly miserable inside because I didn't find it meaningful. Through questioning myself, ideating what I could do differently, and experimenting with all kinds of ideas over five years, I shaped my Noble Work. In this process, the internal dissonance started dissipating.

With Noble Work, this life of congruence is possible for all of us.

CHAPTER 9

Graduating from the Placeholder

THE SEVEN YEARS OF PLACEHOLDER TO NOBLE WORK—ULYSSES S. GRANT

"The fact is I think *I* am a *verb*, instead of a personal pronoun. A verb is anything that signifies to be; to do; to suffer. I signify all three." In mid-July 1885, during the last weeks of his life, Ulysses S. Grant, the Civil War hero and the eighteenth president of the United States, wrote this reflection on his active and tumultuous life.[1] The notion is provocative and inspiring, offering insight into self and how to live.

As you know, the pronoun is a word that stands in place of a noun, such as "I," "me," "we," "you," and "them," and the verb is an action word. Grant was describing that his life was full of actions. He constantly tried doing something throughout his life. He also suffered various misfortunes, including the terminal throat cancer he had when he wrote this note, which led him to death shortly after. But he stayed resilient through many sufferings too. Life is what one can be, do, and bounce back from any unfortunate events, in repeat. Life is never static. We are *verbs*.

Because Ulysses S. Grant has been known as a successful war hero and the US president, we might assume he always wanted to dedicate his life to the military and politics. That wasn't the case. Originally, what he envisioned for himself after graduating from West Point was to become a math teacher. It didn't come true unfortunately, and he stayed in the Army through his twenties.[2]

In 1854, thirty-two-year-old Grant finally left the Army and ventured to do different things. He tried running a wide range of businesses—from farming in plantations to selling firewood, real estate, and leather goods. Unfortunately, none of these attempts were successful, and Grant went back to the Army to lead in the Civil War in 1861, and the rest is history.[3]

Historians assume the direct cause of his resignation from the military commission in 1854 was his excessive drinking. Nonetheless, his seven years of divergence is still noteworthy. Considering Grant's legacy—not only winning the most divisive war in American history but rebuilding the country afterward—it's easy to take that seven years as just an aberration from his military career. However, what if Grant discovered what truly mattered to him through those seven years of experiments?

Let's think about this. For a West Point graduate who had already proved himself with a great track record of leading the Army in the Mexican War, it must have not been easy to put that successful career behind to try something completely different. But he was willing to venture out and pursue a wide range of enterprises.

What would he have learned through those seven years of experiments? He might have learned the hard way that he wasn't good at any civilian businesses. Also, his qualities, such as resilience and perseverance, he cultivated during this period defined his leadership during the Civil War, as he wrote in his memoir.[4] Most of all, this experience would have renewed the meaning of his military career. In 1861, as he decided to participate in the Civil War, he wrote, "Whatever may have been my political opinions before, I have but one sentiment now: That is, we have a government, and laws, and a flag, and they must all be sustained. There are but two parties now: traitors and patriots. And I want hereafter to be ranked with the latter."[5]

We can imagine the meaning of service for Grant got stronger as he came back to the Army after those seven years. Why he wanted to serve the country must have become clearer for him than ever, whether as a leader in the war field or in the White House. Those seven years of Placeholder further defined his Noble Work, based on a clear understanding of what mattered to him, which was to preserve the original values and principles the Founding Fathers set for the United States—still a new country at that time. This clarity would not have been possible without those seven years of ideation and experiments, the Placeholder of his own to be an active verb, not a static pronoun.

JASON'S PLACEHOLDER: "I AM ALWAYS TURNING."
Like many other people I interviewed in this book, I met Jason when I was experimenting hard in my Placeholder. We were in the same boat, both trying a lot of things on the side while also working on our full-time careers at Meta.

Jason participated in an emotional intelligence workshop I facilitated at work, which was one of my many experiments during the Placeholder. In the workshop, Jason resonated with all the topics of emotional intelligence. Seeing a product leader like Jason deeply invested in such a subject was rare, as emotions weren't the virtue most product people I worked with prioritized. I learned he spent additional time on top of his day-to-day work teaching other product managers across the company to build resilience in a turbulent environment like Meta.

With broad shoulders and long hair often tied in a bun, Jason exuded a sense of physicality that I didn't see in many of my colleagues. He trained as a competitive gymnast for sixteen years, ultimately winning a Division 1 NCAA national championship as a student athlete at Stanford. Unfortunately, he suffered a terrible knee injury that cut his athletic career short and had to do a hard pivot. That led him to working in tech companies and founding startups. As a three-time venture-backed founder, Jason had seen success, failure, and everything in between. Through these experiences, he became convinced that learning how to adapt and be resilient was a critical skill to any kind of successful endeavor.

Based on his experiments at Meta, Jason started his own business called Refactor Labs, a modern leadership advisory firm helping leaders and organizations lead through hard pivots. He also wrote a book, *The Path to Pivot*, to serve as a playbook for founders looking to reboot their business. The book is full of his real-life experiences and the many challenges, mistakes, and lessons from his journey. The book is Jason's latest experiment but not the last one for sure.

From an NCAA athlete to a startup founder, product leader, and an executive coach now, Jason has been constantly experimenting to reinvent himself. In a way, the Placeholder mode has always been "on" for him, and he seems pretty even-keeled, riding through different waves in it. What helped him be at ease with the Placeholder? I got curious.

BUILD A SUPPORT SYSTEM FOR FEEDBACK TO EXPERIMENT BETTER

As a product manager, Jason had become data-oriented to evaluate how his products or services were doing. He applied a similar approach to building his own self-awareness by collecting data points about how he was doing with his experiments. He could take many personality or strengths assessment tests, such as Enneagram and StrengthsFinder, to gather and deepen insights about himself. But they were rather passive and only gave him a limited snapshot about his static self. Jason wanted to be more proactive.

So what did he do? He did annual reviews every year with several friends to get more interactive feedback from them. He also invited some mentors or former coworkers with different backgrounds as his personal board of advisors. Jason would keep them up-to-date on what he was doing and regularly invited them to dinner to get their inputs. Also, he worked with different coaches constantly and has been part of a peer coaching group too.

What he did was build a support system around him as a live feedback loop. This stood out in Jason's Placeholder. This system helped Jason evolve his experiments in better directions easily, held him accountable, and kept him honest with his experiments.

Jason couldn't stop speaking of benefits involving other people in the Placeholder in various ways. "Working with other people is super helpful. It creates accountability and perspective. It just feels less heavy to do it than by yourself. I can't just check things off the checklist by myself because it gets really tedious and boring."

Having a healthy feedback network as an external scaffold could be particularly instrumental if you are in a long-term Placeholder mode. Jason points out that they could keep you honest and centered like a solid external hard drive.

> It can be hard to be candid about yourself over time because your memories are often distorted by many other external factors. By engaging with other people and sharing with them how you are evolving, they can call you out in case you are not honest to yourself, saying, "No, Jason, you didn't always think that way. What's changed?" They are like your external hard drive that can reflect your past self like a mirror. That's really important. A coach can do that for you, and so can your friends and communities.

To Jason, everything is an experiment now. His experiments are all different, with varying degrees of importance and scale. All his previous experiences also contributed to his transition to an executive coach. This application of the Placeholder is prolonged and broadened.

Usually, we think of a Placeholder as a limited period of time with a few experiments that resulted in a certain work. That's perfectly fine. But when you are curious about the evolution of what truly matters to you, you might want to continue to ideate, experiment, fine-tune, and iterate like Jason. You come to see everything you do as an experiment. The Placeholder becomes a constant state for you, which is neither good nor bad but is simply another way to understand the Placeholder.

If he were to think of his life in a long line and put all his experiments along that line, they would look like some kind of "turns," which led him to be where he is now. It was completely nonlinear. He didn't and couldn't have planned to be where he is now, so he doesn't try to have a long-term plan for the future either. He has short-term goals in mind that reflect his values and visions, but they work as a tracking measure, not as a final destination.

Jason reflected on this, saying, "Yeah, I think I am always turning. I've been turning for a very long time. As I've gotten older, I now see a longer arc for each turn I make. I am getting comfortable with the fact that I am going to keep turning, and that's okay. Some people only want to reach the destination, but unfortunately, that's not how things go from my experience. I learned that it's okay to keep turning."

Jason recently added a new title to his identity: father. Having welcomed a baby girl into his family, he is turning again toward something new.

WHAT WE DISCOVER IN THE PLACEHOLDER

As you go through your Placeholder, thinking that you are done once you are clear about your Noble Work is natural. That could be true, but you may also realize it's an open end. The exploration never ends as long as you want to grow, which is the true reward of the Placeholder. The reward is not in the final outcome of discovering your Noble Work but in the process of the Placeholder itself, like Jason does.

What else are we discovering in the Placeholder?

1. THINK ORTHOGONALLY ABOUT CAREER

Michael Lewis's *Moneyball: The Art of Winning an Unfair Game* is about how the Oakland Athletics and its general manager, Billy Beane, assembled a competitive team on a small budget using an empirical analysis of data from the in-game activities, called "sabermetrics." Traditionally, in baseball, the statistics such as stolen bases, runs batted in, and batting average were used to assess players. However, Billy Beane thought such an approach was outdated and demonstrated that on-base percentage—how frequently a batter reaches base—and slugging percentage—how productive a batter is in hitting the ball for extra bases—were better metrics.[6]

In this new approach, Beane searched for players who were undervalued in the market, in spite of their higher on-base and slugging percentages. By building the team with this strategy, Oakland Athletics were able to compete effectively with only $44 million for player salaries against teams like New York Yankees, whose payroll exceeded $125 million in the 2002 season. This approach enabled the Athletics to advance to the playoffs in 2002 and 2003 in the most cost-efficient way.[7]

More than the success they achieved, what's fascinating in this story is Billy Beane's perspective to evaluate players' abilities from various angles. For example, for batters to have a higher on-base percentage, they need to advance to the next base as much as possible. The obvious way is getting a hit or hitting a home run, but that's not the only way; you could bunt and steal a base too. Also, how they get a hit, bunt, or steal a base could vary. No one correct way to do it exists. Therefore, he looked for the players who could do it creatively and supported them to grow their idiosyncratic talents within the team.[8] He embraced all kinds of unconventional paths to winning.

This exemplifies orthogonal thinking. In statistics, orthogonal means statistically independent variables that don't seem to affect one another, but in reality, they do.[9] Orthogonal thinking, therefore, means the ability to think beyond what is particularly pertinent to the matter from various angles.

Orthogonal thinking is one of the unexpected gifts waiting for you in the Placeholder. You get to understand you can find different meaningful work over time or in different life stages, and doing so is okay. As your "why" changes, you ideate from orthogonal perspectives you haven't explored before and try new experiments you never did in the past.

Even with your Noble Work, you are not married with a single path to be successful in your career; you are willing to explore different routes. Instead of trying to force fit yourself into a certain mold, you create your own idiosyncratic path. Of course, there are always opportunity costs for whatever track you choose, but you are no longer a hostage of the sunk cost fallacy or the road you didn't take. With orthogonal thinking, you become always ready to reinvent your career, whatever changes may occur.

2. TRULY ACTION-ORIENTED

None of the three critical perspectives of the Placeholder—of an anthropologist, a designer, and a mad scientist—are static; you are not simply planning on paper and daydreaming. As Ulysses S. Grant reflected on his life as a verb, not a pronoun, all these three perspectives for the Placeholder are about actions.

To learn about yourself like an anthropologist, you cannot do it only by thinking about yourself or your work. You need to go through certain experiences to know what matters or doesn't matter to you. That's what everyone I interviewed in this book did; they all learned what was meaningful to them by trying out different roles, jobs, and side projects. Sometimes you'd need to learn unfamiliar ways to reflect on yourself by taking classes, reading, or being challenged by other people in conversations. The reflection exercises I offered are tools that could help you get started with the process of understanding what matters to you. But you need to take action on them to find out what truly matters to you.

The same is true with ideating like a designer; you need to actively seek out new ideas by investing time and effort. Amit in Chapter 5 created his own "Interactive Virtual Lab" to ideate various pathways and asked some of his friends to participate in the process as thought partners. He tried to be open-minded about different ideas proactively until he was able to narrow down to a couple of them that he really wanted to pursue. Ideation is not only thinking but taking actions.

Lastly, experimenting like a mad scientist is definitely all about actions. Julia Child had decade-long experiments from 1951 to 1961, until she published the book *Mastering the Art of French Cooking*, which officially set off her career as a chef. Jason took so many actions from working in different industries and roles to founding companies, starting his own blog, and writing a book. His experiments are still going on.

The quintessence of the Placeholder is "action." Herminia Ibarra, the professor of leadership and career transition at London Business School, emphasized the actions people took in major transformations in their careers. Describing the unconventional nature of career change, she says we learn who we are and discover new possibilities by doing—by trying out new activities and interacting with new people and integrating new insights to shape and clarify who we are becoming.[10]

As you go through your Placeholder, you are working on launching yourselves anew. Doing so is as if you are sculpting a shape out of a big piece of amorphous marble or painting a picture of your future. The inspiration for what you'd like to create doesn't suddenly strike you like thunder, but you come to know it little by little through countless chiseling or sketches, like "flesh and blood examples, concrete experiments," as told by Ibarra.[11] As you learned through three perspectives of the Placeholder, you need to get curious, envision, explore, and experiment. Ibarra writes, "Working identity is above all a practice: a never-ending process of putting ourselves through a set of knowable steps that creates and reveals our possible selves."[12]

A truly action-oriented mindset is what's waiting for you in the Placeholder. You become more flexible, ready, and unafraid to experiment, whether it's small or big.

3. APPRECIATE THE PROCESS AS THE PRIZE: JILL'S PLACEHOLDER

We all know the law of diminishing returns.[13] After you finally get the car or house you were dreaming of, the satisfaction or utility derived from it decreases. The same applies to the dream job you thought would make you the happiest person on Earth; it would become like any other jobs you had in the past after a while.

This law doesn't apply to the Placeholder and Noble Work because the satisfaction and fulfillment comes from the Placeholder experience itself, not the work you do as an outcome. As you stay open to the journey of growth and exploration, facing all kinds of unexpected challenges in the process, you get to unlock the *prolonging* returns.

Jill Berkowitz had been teaching in a middle school for thirteen years when she started feeling burnout and lack of joy in her work. She was always told that she'd make a great teacher since childhood. Teaching was her dream job for thirteen years, but she couldn't dismiss the signal of languishing. Jill began digging deeper into the question of "What do I want to do now?"

One of the ideas was to try doing something with writing. Throughout her entire career, writing was one coherent thing Jill liked and was good at. She was trained to write as a journalism major in college, worked at a publishing company reviewing many manuscripts of writers before being a teacher, and taught writing in schools. Jill initiated exploring any jobs where she could use her writing skills.

At the outset, Jill had a lot of headwinds; she was not up-to-date with the latest job market after working as a teacher for thirteen years, which almost became her identity. But it didn't discourage her; she was open to learning new ways. Her friend suggested freelancing as a writer instead of looking for a specific job that was taking too long to find. *Why not?* She uploaded her résumé to Upwork, a platform for freelancers finding work.

The process was long and arduous. At first, for all the gigs she applied for on Upwork, Jill usually received rejections or no response. Whenever her patience wore thin, Jill remembered the story of Wendy Mass, the famous children's book writer. One day, Wendy Mass came to speak at Jill's school. During her talk, she threw out a big scroll of papers long enough to roll down the aisle, all the way back to the auditorium. It turned out to be every rejection letter Wendy Mass has received from publishers, which she kept. When Jill was getting a series of rejections on Upwork, she reminded herself of Wendy's story. "Even Wendy Mass, the *New York Times* children's book bestseller author, got all those rejection letters before she found the right publisher who appreciated her work eventually!"

As Jill didn't give up and kept applying, she got some gigs as a freelance writer for various projects and started building up her portfolio of work. One day, she applied for another freelance gig at a tech startup that looked interesting. Without overthinking, she applied for it with a short cover letter and some sample work.

That night, they wrote back to her and hired her for a project. They liked her work so much they wanted to offer her full-time employment. Now, Jill is working full-time at this startup, educating their clients about the products through various communication channels. As a middle school teacher who reinvented herself to lead content for a tech startup, Jill is a remarkable example of a career changer. She finds her current work so meaningful, but Jill feels more rewarded by the process itself. She reflected in the interview:

> I always found it odd that, in this culture, we are obsessed about one perfect career or one perfect purpose for us in life. But what if there isn't or there are multiple of them? Through my experience in the Placeholder, I would like to motivate people that it's okay to feel something you are doing is not the right thing for you anymore. It's okay to do something different, drastically different like mine. I think that's my Noble Work—to educate people with this concept.

Today, Jill is focused on creating and managing content for a high-growth tech startup while actively sharing her insights as a career change advocate based on her experiences, inspiring many others who might have a similar urge as she did. Jill is enjoying the process of evolving her potential as an educator into different forms and contexts.

Seeing that the biggest reward lies in the process is also what's waiting for you in the Placeholder.

The Placeholder has no end goal; hence, no graduation. Disappointed? Sorry, but this is true. This anticlimactic quality of the Placeholder reminds me of meditation. My meditation teachers always say we don't meditate to get enlightened or to reach nirvana; we simply meditate and welcome whatever happens in the process. But even though the end point doesn't really exist for either meditation or the Placeholder, I think both teach us the way of living a good life.

What do I mean by a *good life*? I am certainly not talking about having more money, power, status, or achievements, as these values are transient in life. The psychologist Carl Rogers writes, "The good life is a process, not a state of being."[14] A good life is about how we live this tumultuous, unpredictable, and nonlinear life. This isn't a static goal to achieve. "It involves the stretching and growing of becoming more and more of one's potentialities," as Carl Rogers notes.[15]

This brings us back to the Placeholder. The Placeholder is a widening circle of learning about ourselves, growing out of our comfort zone ideas, and applying ourselves to them over and over. Through it, we come to create our Noble Work that enables us and others to be fully human in this ever-unfolding outward spiral. It's not easy, but as Carl Rogers observes, "Yet the deeply exciting thing about human beings is that when the individual is inwardly free, he chooses as the good life this process of becoming."[16]

Life can be joyful, but it's also challenging. Life is full of great moments but also painful ones. Through practicing meditation every day, we are pleasantly surprised to discover we are a little less frustrated by unexpected events life presents often. After going through the Placeholder, it is invigorating to know the extreme uncertainty with our career doesn't scare us as much anymore. With this sense of equanimity and gumption, we can take any challenges in this process of becoming.

With the Placeholder, we might not graduate from anything, but we come to graduate *to* this good life.

Conclusion

The book I was thinking about writing back in January 2024 was different from the one I am finishing writing now. At first, I focused on Noble Work. My goal-driven mindset I got so accustomed to in my whole life favored the end result rather than the process. It seemed more exciting and meaningful. The Placeholder? Meh, it's just a tedious, confusing, and grueling process. Not so sexy. Focus on the prize, not how you get the prize!

This changed dramatically once I started writing. As I looked back on the Placeholder experiences of my own and my interviewees, I realized how we go through the Placeholder was not only more interesting, but that's also the real deal. Going through the Placeholder is not a mere process or a means to an end. Through the Placeholder, we all learn that feeling a bit lost and not knowing what we are supposed to do as the next act is okay. We get to accept our idiosyncratic and uncertain paths and go even further to learn how to enjoy this iterative process of reinventing ourselves without anxiety and worry.

The Placeholder, as it turns out, is a great playground to learn and practice self-awareness, growth mindset, grit, self-compassion, creativity, and more. The Placeholder is a container of important qualities for the good life that many self-help book authors, famous psychologists, and organization development experts are spotlighting. This is the prize. Plus, you can get a nice bonus—your own Noble Work.

Of course, I was not aware of all these benefits when I entered my own Placeholder. Can you imagine how nice it would have been though, if I knew what I know now about the Placeholder? I could have been a little more patient and guided myself better for a different "test" I needed to run. I would have been less critical of myself, with less anxiety and worry, and been better engaged with my work and people around me. So I wrote this book because I hope you don't suffer as much as I did in the Placeholder. I want you to know that feeling lost and uncertain about your next act is completely okay.

*****

While working on this book in the fall of 2024, I spent a lot of time in Korea with my dad. He was dying from terminal cancer, and I knew his time with us was limited. One day, he asked me to look for an old magazine from one of the bookshelves in his apartment. He had a photographic memory of where it was in the middle of thousands of books he owned. "I want you to keep it safe because it's very important for me," he told me in a trembling voice.

The magazine was from 1966. The entire cover had turned yellow, and all the colors were faded. The binding was falling apart with loose pages throughout. It was a famous literary magazine for high school students in the 1960s in Korea. My dad, who was in high school then, wrote a short story, and it was selected and published in that magazine.

I flipped through the brittle pages very carefully to look for his story. There he was in a small black-and-white photo of his nineteen-year-old self. He looked a bit anxious and serious in a school uniform. What he wrote was a coming-of-age story about an orphaned boy from the Korean war. The critics of the magazine said in their review of my dad's work that they appreciated his sincere effort to understand the poignancy of life. Since then, he had dreamed of becoming a novelist.

His love for books and writing continued through his college, and he worked as an editor in chief for the university paper too. Eventually, he became a journalist and worked for several newspaper companies as an editor in chief and columnist. He wrote columns almost every day over thirty years about various topics—from political to social and cultural issues in Korea. With those columns and essays, he also published five books. His life was full of books and writing he had loved since he was young.

A couple of years ago, when he finally retired from his post as a columnist, I asked him what he wanted to do for the rest of his life, now finally free from his daily writing duty. Without hesitation, he answered, "I want to write a good novel before I die. That's always what I wanted to do, but I was too busy to pull that off." I asked him if he had a story in mind. He smiled and said, "Oh, I have many stories to write about…"

On November 1, 2024, about a month after he asked me to take care of the magazine with his first fiction published, he died. He was seventy-seven. After his funeral, I opened up that magazine again and read what he said in the interview about his short story being selected by the magazine. He said, "For a long time, I doubted myself as a novelist. I wasn't sure if I deserved to be it. I am so grateful for this recognition because it encourages me to keep writing stories no matter what. That will prove me as a novelist."

Reading it, I felt so bad about what might have stopped him from writing the novel he always wanted to write. As an editor in chief, columnist, eldest son, brother, husband, and father, he had so many responsibilities. He liked his career though. He dedicated his entire life to it and had achieved a lot. But I couldn't help but wonder, *Would he have regretted not writing a novel?*

One day after the funeral, I discovered his journal among his possessions. This surprised me because he didn't write much personally since he had to write every day for work. I never got any letters or Christmas cards, let alone emails from him. The journal started with an entry about his reflection as he was about to retire, just a couple of years ago. He wrote how strange it was to not write every day and also made a long list of things he wanted to do in his free time.

Then I discovered many little notes he scribbled on the journal. They were notes about some news he watched on TV or what he read in books. Other notes were about his thoughts around some political events or social issues. I realized they were recollections for whatever he was going to write about in the future. Seeing them was familiar to me, as I grew up discovering those random notes here and there scribbled in his handwriting around the house.

What was this for? He didn't have to write his columns anymore, I wondered. Only then did it hit me; the notes were for the very first novel he always wanted to write.

He still remembered what started his writing career fifty-nine years ago. At age seventy-seven, he was willing to give it a shot and try reinventing himself as the novelist he always wanted to be. Holding the journal, I broke down crying.

Life without regret is impossible. Such is probably the ultimate dream of perfectionists, but we all know perfectionism is a mirage. I don't claim we get to live a regret-proof life through the Placeholder by creating Noble Work we find truly meaningful. That would be a lie.

But I do believe in the power of our intrinsic motivation, which drives us for self-actualization and transcendence.[1] My dad was trying to do that. Although it might have been a small change from a newspaper columnist to a novelist, it meant a big shift for him to finally attempt to dedicate himself to something he valued so much since he was nineteen years old.

Life is too short to suppress those needs and live in the status quo or inertia when everything inside and outside us changes. Trying to change from what you have been doing for ten, fifteen, or twenty years to something completely new could be terrifying. But with the Placeholder, you can think of it as *different*, not difficult. It will become *difficult* if you try to keep doing the same thing, even though you know it doesn't serve you anymore.

I hope you don't hesitate to enter the Placeholder. Instead, I hope you can gladly accept the invitation to the Placeholder and start the adventure full of rich insights about yourself, fun and unfamiliar ideas you never tried, and dynamic experiments you will learn so much from. Although it might feel dangerous and unfamiliar at times, I want you to know you are safe on this journey. When it feels difficult, remember that it's just *different* from what you have done before.

May this book help you stay courageous in your Placeholder, to find your own peace and balance with work toward a good life.

Acknowledgments

Writing this book was a great practice not aiming for perfection but "good enough." Yet, even achieving that good enough was a big task, which would have been impossible without the help of so many people.

First, I'd like to thank my interviewees, who generously shared their stories and were willing to become part of this book. Gregory Kim, Heather Pollock, Jason Shen, Jenn Yee, Jill Berkowitz, Joshua Steinfeldt, Judy Huang, Steph Stern, and Vijay Natarajan: Thank you so much for your generosity for sharing your Placeholder experiences. Even those of you whose stories weren't selected for this book after all, I am deeply thankful to you. Your courage to walk through your own Placeholders is so inspiring. Thank you.

Secondly, one hundred supporters backed this project to be possible by contributing to the preorder of the book in advance. I want to acknowledge all of your names here—first name in alphabetical order—to show my deepest gratitude for believing in me and the premise of this book. Your generosity made it possible to turn an idea into this book.

Aaron Culich, Adriana Henao, Aileen Cureton, Aisling Scott, Amit Patel, Amy Connors, Anna Nygren, Anya Smith, Arya Paturkar, Audrey Yi, Belen Juri, Bob Peck, Chris Catania, Chris Harrison, Claire Currie, Clara Lee, Claudia Fernandes, Colleen Myers, Craig Souza, Dadalei Buth, Daniel James, Daranne Harris, Darren Pham, David Glen, Dean Fealk, Debora Gama Lima, Elizabeth Liu, Enrique Stiglich, Eric Koester, Fernanda Davila Melo Sarmento, Francesca

Leonetti, Francisco Varela, Grace Jimenez, Greg Leung, Gregory Kim, Hanming Wang, Hiral Parekh, Hyunjoo Lee, Inci Wittig, Iris Chae, James Regan, Janice Lin, Jason Shen, Jennifer Liu, Jennifer Yturralde, Jennifer Slawson, Jenny Fong, Jessica Yau, Jieun Lee, Karlo Teran, Kelly Grimaldi, Kenny and Kristin Kim, Lauren Lee, Lenn Pryor, Lily Lyman, Luana Matos, Maria Antonia Hernandez, Mark Blackburn, Matt Garlick, Matthew Stevens, Meg Moore, Megha Maripuri, Michael Park, Mindy Zhang, Newsha Taheri, Nicole Mesko, Noori Kim, Oh Young Koo, Oliver Ross, Pamela Sedano, Pavan Singh, Phillip Lee, Phillipe Han, Rachell Morris, Raghav Mathur, Ran Makavy, Randy Wagner, Roger Greene, Ron Sebahar, Sarah Hunt, Shahid Hussain, Shahzeb Zakaria, Stephen Morse, Sujin Choi, Suzanne Trimmer, Tad Wakasugi, Tania Trapla, Tebeen Ibrahim, Toma Pigli, Tricia Kim, Vanessa Abram, Vijay Natarajan, Vikash Raniga, Vincent Gonguet, Yu Lee Kim—THANK YOU.

Third, I'd like to thank the Manuscripts LLC community for discovering my ideas of Placeholder and Noble Work and supporting me to transform them into this book. Until I started writing this, I thought writing a book was mainly a solitary experience, like me sitting alone with my computer and just writing. I was dead wrong; the process was highly collaborative, with so many people involved. Together, they poured so much time and care into taking my idea to become this book. Looking back, this process equates to growing a big tree out of a mere seed.

Thank you so much Eric Koester for planting the seeds in me about this book, Angela Murray for helping me sprout the seeds, Angela Ivey for your encouragement to help me grow new shoots to become a baby tree, Zach Marcum for coaching me on how to grow the tree, Zen Grabs for advising me to better take care of this tree, Ken Cain for holding me accountable with nurturing this tree to become stronger and bigger, and Stephanie McKibben for your ongoing support with natural fertilizers for this tree.

Lastly, I honestly don't believe I could have done this without my biggest cheerleaders in life: my family. First and foremost, my husband, Daniel Morris: Thank you so much for always reminding me who I am becoming with your unwavering love. My stepdaughter, Ozzie Morris: Thank you for entering my life and expanding my love to the level I never knew. And my late father, who happened to be the very first writer in my life, Byung-Gil Kim: Dad, I am forever thankful to you for inspiring me to be a writer. I wrote this for you.

Notes

INTRODUCTION

1. "Lorem Ipsum," *Lorem Ipsum*, accessed January 8, 2025, https://www.lipsum.com.

CHAPTER 1

1. Jeff Selingo, "The Rise of the Double Major," *Next* (blog), *The Chronicle of Higher Education*, October 11, 2012, https://www.chronicle.com/blogs/next/the-worrying-rise-of-double-majors.
2. Paul A. O'Keefe, Carol S. Dweck, and Gregory M. Walton, "Implicit Theories of Interest: Finding Your Passion or Developing It?" *Psychological Science* 29, no. 10 (September 2018): 1653–1664, https://doi.org/10.1177/0956797618780643.
3. Ibid.
4. Adam Smith, *An Inquiry into the Nature and Causes of the Wealth of Nations*, ed. Edwin Cannan (New York: Random House, 1994).
5. Ibid.
6. Adam Smith, *An Inquiry into the Nature and Causes of the Wealth of Nations*, ed. Edwin Cannan (New York: Random House, 1994).
7. Ford Motor Company, "The Moving Assembly Line and the Five-Dollar Workday," *History* (blog), *Ford Motor Company*, 2024, accessed January 15, 2025, https://corporate.ford.com/articles/history/moving-assembly-line.html.
8. CCA Partners, "CCA | State of the Global Workplace: 2022 Report," *Gallup* (blog), *CCA*, https://www.cca-global.com/content/latest/article/2023/05/state-of-the-global-workplace-2022-report-346/.

9. Gallup, *State of the Global Workplace*, (New Mexico: Gallup, 2024), https://www.gallup.com/workplace/349484/state-of-the-global-workplace.aspx.
10. Drew Carey, "I Hate My Job," Dvsbstrd, April 14, 2010, 00:19:46, https://www.youtube.com/watch?v=Ph9I-qPQ6FU.
11. Adam Smith, *An Inquiry into the Nature and Causes of the Wealth of Nations*, ed. Edwin Cannan (New York: Random House, 1994).
12. Barry Schwartz, *Why We Work* (New York: Simon & Schuster/TED, 2015).
13. *Working: What We Do All Day*, directed by Caroline Suh (2023; Concordia Studio, 2023), 00:47:49, Netflix documentary, https://www.netflix.com/watch/81261205.

CHAPTER 2

1. Jim Harter, "Is Quiet Quitting Real?" *Workplace* (blog), *Gallup.com*, September 6, 2022, https://www.gallup.com/workplace/398306/quiet-quitting-real.aspx.
2. Ibid.
3. Gallup, *State of the Global Workplace*, (New Mexico: Gallup, 2024), https://www.gallup.com/workplace/349484/state-of-the-global-workplace.aspx.
4. Ibid.
5. Gallup, *State of the Global Workplace*, (New Mexico: Gallup, 2024), https://www.gallup.com/workplace/349484/state-of-the-global-workplace.aspx.
6. World Bank Group, "GDP (Current US$)," 2025, accessed January 10, 2025, https://data.worldbank.org/indicator/NY.GDP.MKTP.CD.
7. Adam Grant, "How to Stop Languishing and Start Finding Flow," August 2021, Monterey, TED video, 00:15:50, https://www.ted.com/talks/adam_grant_how_to_stop_languishing_and_start_finding_flow.
8. Corey Keyes, *Languishing: How to Feel Alive Again in a World That Wears Us Down* (London: Transworld, 2024).

9. Gallup, *State of the Global Workplace*, (New Mexico: Gallup, 2024), https://www.gallup.com/workplace/349484/state-of-the-global-workplace.aspx.
10. Dennis Nørmark and Anders Fogh Jensen, *Pseudowork: How We Ended Up Being Busy Doing Nothing*, trans. Tam McTurk (Copenhagen, Denmark: Gyldendal, 2021).
11. Ibid.
12. Ann Kellett, "The Texas A&M Professor Who Predicted 'The Great Resignation,'" *Culture & Society* (blog) *Texas A&M Today*, February 11, 2022, https://today.tamu.edu/2022/02/11/the-texas-am-professor-who-predicted-the-great-resignation/.
13. AJ Hess, "The Professor Who Coined 'The Great Resignation' Says It's Finally Over. Here's What's Next," *The Future of Work* (blog), *Fast Company*, 2025, accessed January 29, 2025, https://www.fastcompany.com/90932493/the-professor-who-coined-the-term-the-great-resignation-says-it-is-finally-over.
14. Ethan Bernstein, Michael B. Horn, and Bob Moesta, *Job Moves: 9 Steps for Making Progress in Your Career* (New York: HarperCollins, 2024).
15. Ibid.
16. Roger Lee, "Layoffs Tracker," n.d., accessed January 15, 2025, https://layoffs.fyi.
17. Population and Housing Unit Estimates, "Tables," United States Census Bureau, n.d., accessed January 20, 2025, https://data.census.gov/all?q=Boston%20city,%20Massachusetts.
18. Roger Lee, "Layoffs Tracker," n.d., accessed January 15, 2025, https://layoffs.fyi.
19. Adecco Group, *What Is the True Impact of AI at Work?* (Zürich, Switzerland: Adecco Group, 2024), https://www.adeccogroup.com/future-of-work/latest-insights/what-is-the-true-impact-of-ai-at-work.
20. Daniel H. Pink, *Drive: The Surprising Truth About What Motivates Us* (London: Penguin, 2011).
21. Ibid.
22. Merriam-Webster.com Dictionary, s.v. "autotelic," accessed January 17, 2025, https://www.merriam-webster.com/dictionary/autotelic.

23. Daniel H. Pink, *Drive: The Surprising Truth About What Motivates Us* (London: Penguin, 2011).
24. Ibid.
25. Daniel H. Pink, *Drive: The Surprising Truth About What Motivates Us* (London: Penguin, 2011).
26.
    a. 3M, "3M's 15% Culture," *3M Careers* (blog), *3M.co.uk*, 2025, accessed January 17, 2025, https://www.3m.co.uk/3M/en_GB/careers/culture/15-percent-culture/.
    b. Dorie Clark, "Google's '20% Rule' Shows Exactly How Much Time You Should Spend Learning New Skills—and Why It Works, Success," *Success* (blog), *CNBC*, December 16, 2021, https://www.cnbc.com/2021/12/16/google-20-percent-rule-shows-exactly-how-much-time-you-should-spend-learning-new-skills.html.
    a. Mike Cannon-Brookes, "Atlassian's 20% Time Experiment," *Products & News* (blog), *Atlassian*, March 10, 2008, https://www.atlassian.com/blog/archives/20_time_experiment$.
27. Daniel H. Pink, *Drive: The Surprising Truth About What Motivates Us* (London: Penguin, 2011).
28. Bryan Goodwin and Kirsten B. Miller, "Research Says/Creativity Requires a Mix of Skills," *ASCD* (blog), February 1, 2013, https://ascd.org/el/articles/creativity-requires-a-mix-of-skills.
29. Teresa Amabile, *Creativity in Context: Update to the Social Psychology of Creativity* (Boulder, CO: Westview Press, 1996).
30. Nicole Celestine, "Abraham Maslow, His Theory & Contribution to Psychology," *Theory & Books* (blog), *PositivePsychology.com*, September 29, 2017, https://positivepsychology.com/abraham-maslow/.
31. Douglas McGregor, *The Human Side of Enterprise* (New York: McGraw Hill, 2016).
32. Richard M. Ryan and Edward L. Deci, "Self-Determination Theory and the Facilitation of Intrinsic Motivation, Social Development, and Well-Being," *American Psychologist* 55, no. 1 (2000): 68–78, https://doi.org/10.1037/0003-066X.55.1.68.

CHAPTER 3

1. "Design Thinking (DT)," *Topics* (blog), *Interaction Design Foundation*, n.d., accessed January 31, 2025, https://www.interaction-design.org/literature/topics/design-thinking.
2. Ibid.
3. "Design Thinking (DT)," *Topics* (blog), *Interaction Design Foundation*, n.d., accessed January 31, 2025, https://www.interaction-design.org/literature/topics/design-thinking.
4. Ibid.

CHAPTER 4

1. Gabriel Andrade, "René Girard (1923–2015)," n.d., accessed January 11, 2025. https://iep.utm.edu/girard/.
2. René Girard, *Deceit, Desire, and the Novel: Self and Other in Literary Structure* (Baltimore, MD: Johns Hopkins University Press, 1976).
3. Ibid.
4. Viktor E. Frankl, *Man's Search for Meaning* (Boston, MA: Beacon Press, 2006).
5. Indiana University of Pennsylvania Department of Anthropology, *Introduction to Anthropology: Holistic and Applied Research on Being Human* (Indiana, PA: Indiana University of Pennsylvania, 2022), https://www.iup.edu/ages/files/anthropology/research/oer03.pdf.
6. Anthroholic, "Participant Observation," last updated 2025, accessed January 15, 2015, https://anthroholic.com/participant-observation.
7. Ibid.
8. Marcus Aurelius, *Meditations*, trans. Martin Hammond (New York: Penguin, 2015).

CHAPTER 5

1. Viktor E. Frankl, *Man's Search for Meaning* (Boston, MA: Beacon Press, 2006).
2. John Cleese, "John Cleese on Creativity in Management," *Video Arts*, released January 23, 1991, 00:36:59, https://youtu.be/Pb5oIIPO62g.

3. James Clear, "Creativity in Management," *James Clear* (blog), n.d., accessed January 31, 2025, https://jamesclear.com/great-speeches/creativity-in-management-by-john-cleese.
4. John Cleese, "John Cleese on Creativity in Management," *Video Arts*, released January 23, 1991, 00:36:59, https://youtu.be/Pb5oIIPO62g.
5. Ibid.
6. John Cleese, "John Cleese on Creativity in Management," *Video Arts*, released January 23, 1991, 00:36:59, https://youtu.be/Pb5oIIPO62g.
7. Graham Wallas, *The Art of Thought* (Dorset, England: Solis Press, 2018).
8. Kate DiCamillo, *The Magician's Elephant* (Somerville, MA: Candlewick Press, 2009).
9. Designing Your Life, "Design the Most Important Project of All: Your Life," last updated 2025, accessed January 13, 2025, https://designingyour.life.
10. Bill Burnett and Dave Evans, *Designing Your Life: How to Build a Well-Lived, Joyful Life* (New York: Knopf Doubleday Publishing Group, 2016).
11. Steven P. Dow, Alana Glassco, Jonathan Kass, Melissa Schwarz, Daniel L. Schwartz, and Scott R. Klemmer, "Parallel Prototyping Leads to Better Design Results, More Divergence, and Increased Self-Efficacy," *ACM Transactions on Computer-Human Interaction (TOCHI)* 17, no. 4 (December 2010): 1–24, https://doi.org/10.1145/1879831.1879836.

CHAPTER 6

1. *The Curious Case of Benjamin Button*, directed by David Fincher (2008; Paramount Pictures, December 25, 2008), 02:46:00, DVD, https://www.imdb.com/title/tt0421715/.
2. *The Secret Life of Walter Mitty*, directed by Ben Stiller (2013; Samuel Goldwyn Films, December 25, 2013), 01:54:00, DVD, https://www.imdb.com/title/tt0359950/.
3. Ibid.
4. *The Secret Life of Walter Mitty*, directed by Ben Stiller (2013; Samuel Goldwyn Films, December 25, 2013), 01:54:00, DVD, https://www.imdb.com/title/tt0359950/.

5. Stefan Van Der Stigchel, *Concentration: Staying Focused in Times of Distraction*, trans. Danny Guinan (Cambridge, MA: MIT Press, 2020).
6. Matthew A. Killingsworth and Daniel T. Gilbert, "A Wandering Mind Is an Unhappy Mind," *Science* 330, no. 6006 (November 2010): 932, https://www.science.org/doi/10.1126/science.1192439.
7. Ibid.
8. Michael S. Franklin, Michael D. Mrazek, Craig L. Anderson, Jonathan Smallwood, Alan Kingstone, and Jonathan W. Schooler, "The Silver Lining of a Mind in the Clouds: Interesting Musings Are Associated with Positive Mood while Mind-Wandering," *Frontiers in Psychology* 4 (August 2013): 583, https://doi.org/10.3389/fpsyg.2013.00583.
9. Bob Spitz, *Dearie: The Remarkable Life of Julia Child* (New York: Knopf, 2012).
10.
    a. Bob Spitz, *Dearie* (New York: Penguin Random House, 2013).
    b. Julia Child and Alex Prud'homme, *My Life in France* (New York: Knopf Doubleday Publishing Group, 2007).
    c. Noel Riley Fitch, *Appetite for Life: The Biography of Julia Child* (New York: Knopf Doubleday Publishing Group, 2012).
11. Ibid.
12.
    a. Bob Spitz, *Dearie* (New York: Penguin Random House, 2013).
    b. Julia Child and Alex Prud'homme, *My Life in France* (New York: Knopf Doubleday Publishing Group, 2007).
    c. Noel Riley Fitch, *Appetite for Life: The Biography of Julia Child* (New York: Knopf Doubleday Publishing Group, 2012).
13. Ibid.
14.
    a. Bob Spitz, *Dearie* (New York: Penguin Random House, 2013).
    b. Noel Riley Fitch, *Appetite for Life: The Biography of Julia Child* (New York: Knopf Doubleday Publishing Group, 2012).
15. Daniel Schlagwein, "The History of Digital Nomadism" (PDF, International Workshop on the Changing Nature of Work, December 6,

2018), https://www.researchgate.net/publication/329182172_The_History_of_Digital_Nomadism.

16. Dan Pilat, "Why Do Unpredictable Events Only Seem Predictable After They Occur?" *The Decision Lab* (blog), 2025, accessed February 1, 2025, https://thedecisionlab.com/biases/hindsight-bias.

17. Neal J. Roese and Kathleen D. Vohs, "Hindsight Bias," *Perspectives on Psychological Science* 7, no. 5 (September 2012): 411–426, https://doi.org/10.1177/1745691612454303.

CHAPTER 7

1. N. Gregory Mankiw, *Principles of Microeconomics* (Boston, MA: Cengage Learning, 2008).
2. Shirzad Chamine, *Positive Intelligence: Why Only 20% of Teams and Individuals Achieve Their True Potential and How You Can Achieve Yours* (Austin, TX: Greenleaf Book Group Press, 2016).

CHAPTER 8

1. Merriam-Webster.com Dictionary, s.v. "noble," accessed January 17, 2025, https://www.merriam-webster.com/dictionary/noble.
2. Albert Bandura, *Self-Efficacy: The Exercise of Control* (New York: Worth Publishers, 1997).
3. Ibid.
4. Albert Bandura, *Self-Efficacy: The Exercise of Control* (New York: Worth Publishers, 1997).
5. Joseph Walters and Howard Gardner, *The Crystallizing Experience: Discovering an Intellectual Gift* (Cambridge, MA: Harvard Project Zero, 1984), https://eric.ed.gov/?id=ED254544.
6. Abraham H. Maslow, "A Theory of Human Motivation," *Psychological Review* 50, no. 4 (1943): 370–396, https://doi.org/10.1037/h0054346.
7. Ibid.
8. Scott Barry Kaufman, *Transcend: The New Science of Self-Actualization* (New York: Penguin, 2020).
9. Ibid.

CHAPTER 9

1. John Y. Simon, *The Papers of Ulysses S. Grant, Volume 31: January 1, 1883–July 23, 1885* (Carbondale, IL: Southern Illinois University Press, 2009).
2. "Ulysses S. Grant Biographies," *Biographies* (blog), *National Museum of the United States Army*, 2025, accessed January 19, 2025, https://www.thenmusa.org/biographies/ulysses-s-grant/.
3. Ibid.
4. Ulysses S. Grant, *The Personal Memoirs of U.S. Grant* (New York: Charles L. Webster and Company, 1885).
5. "Ulysses S. Grant Biographies," *Biographies* (blog), *National Museum of the United States Army*, 2025, accessed January 19, 2025, https://www.thenmusa.org/biographies/ulysses-s-grant/.
6. Michael Lewis, *Moneyball: The Art of Winning an Unfair Game* (New York: W. W. Norton & Company, 2003).
7. Ibid.
8. Michael Lewis, *Moneyball: The Art of Winning an Unfair Game* (New York: W. W. Norton & Company, 2003).
9. Athanasios Papoulis and S. Unnikrishna Pillai, *Probability, Random Variables, and Stochastic Processes* (New York: McGraw Hill, 2002).
10. Herminia Ibarra, *Working Identity: Unconventional Strategies for Reinventing Your Career* (Boston, MA: Harvard Business Press, 2004).
11. Ibid.
12. Herminia Ibarra, *Working Identity: Unconventional Strategies for Reinventing Your Career* (Boston, MA: Harvard Business Press, 2004).
13. *Britannica Money* (2025), s.v. "diminishing returns," https://www.britannica.com/money/diminishing-returns.
14. Carl Rogers, *On Becoming a Person: A Therapist's View on Psychotherapy, Humanistic Psychology, and the Path to Personal Growth* (San Francisco, CA: HarperOne, September 7, 1995).
15. Ibid.

16. Carl Rogers, *On Becoming a Person: A Therapist's View on Psychotherapy, Humanistic Psychology, and the Path to Personal Growth* (San Francisco, CA: HarperOne, September 7, 1995).

CONCLUSION

1. Abraham Maslow, *Critique of Self-Actualization Theory*, ed. Edward Hoffman (Thousand Oaks, CA: Sage Publications, 1996).